HISTORIC TOWNS OF ENGLAND

in *Pictures*

WITH AN INTRODUCTION BY
BRIAN VESEY-FITZGERALD

CONTENTS

*

INTRODUCTION
page 5

NORTH COUNTRY
page 13

MIDLAND ENGLAND
page 31

THE WEST COUNTRY
page 53

SOUTH-WEST ENGLAND
page 71

SOUTH-EAST ENGLAND
page 93

ODHAMS PRESS LTD · LONG ACRE, LONDON

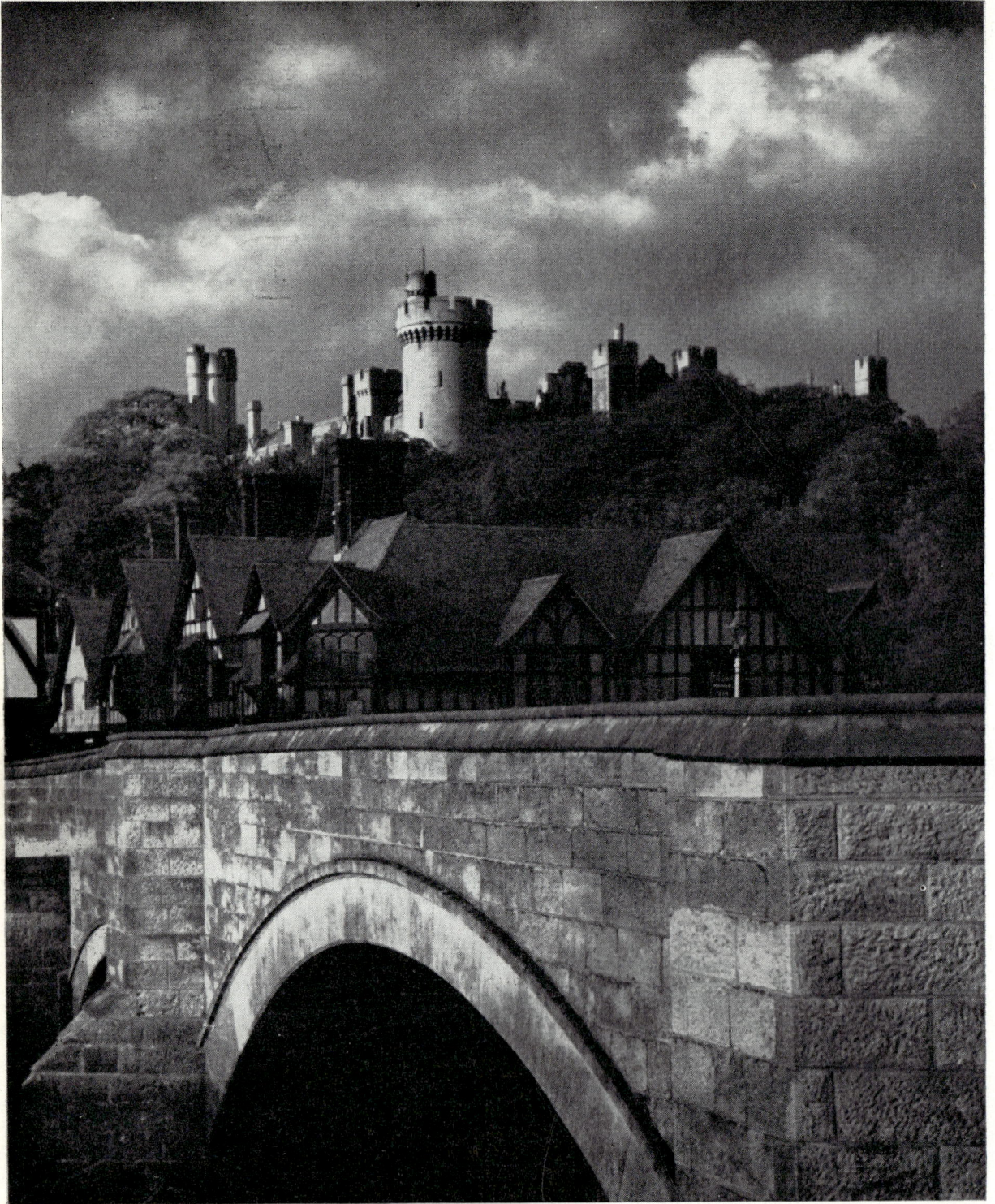

THE CASTLE AND TOWN OF ARUNDEL FROM THE ARUN RIVER

HISTORIC TOWNS
OF ENGLAND
in Pictures

THE ROMAN BATH AND THE ABBEY OF BATH

942-84

Introduction

WE take our towns for granted. We take for granted the cathedral or the parish church, the cross at the town centre, the smells and bustle of market, the election of the Mayor, the annual procession of Mayor and Corporation to church, even the cobblestones that still survive here and there. We are so accustomed to the sights and sounds of English country towns, so familiar with them that we scarcely pause to think about them.

If we were to pause and reflect upon these things that we know so well, we should find revealed for us a vista stretching back through the years, in many cases to the very beginnings of our history. The parish church may well have been an abbey before the Dissolution of the Monasteries, and at the time of that primitive experiment in nationalization may have been bought from Henry VIII by the town with monies subscribed by the townsfolk: the market may be held under a charter granted by Henry III or even, in some exceptional cases, by William the Conqueror: the cathedral may well owe its origin to the work of some Celtic missionary saint: the town itself may have been planned by the Romans.

Indeed, many of the oldest and most historic of our towns do date from the time when most of England was a Roman province. Of course, there were towns in England long before the Romans came. Maiden Castle in Dorset was once, presumably, a town—certainly, it was a centre of population—and Avebury in Wiltshire, now little more than a hamlet, was one of the densest centres of population in prehistoric England. But places such as these, busy and thriving though they undoubtedly were, cannot be considered towns in the modern sense: they possessed no architecture and, so far as one can tell, no plan other than that of the defensive perimeter.

The first planning of our towns, the first establishment of civic life and civic authority, is purely a Roman achievement. Many of the Roman sites, which have been classified as towns, were selected solely for military reasons and were really fortified camps without a civic life. A large number of these are today no more than villages; many are no more than names on a map. But military strategy was not the only consideration that governed the Roman choice of site. Many of these Roman towns were placed close to, or actually on the site of, earlier settlements, for the simple reason that there was already in being a centre of population. Here the governing factor was both military and commercial. For the same reasons (defence and commerce) towns sprang up along the roads; the great straight roads,

5

many of which are in use to this day, memorials to the skill of Roman engineers. Communications were of supreme importance, and it is along the great trunk roads—Watling Street, Stane Street, Ermine Street, Akeman Street, the Fosse Way—and particularly at the points where these and other important roads joined or crossed that the large towns—Alcester, Chester, Cirencester, Exeter, Leicester, Lincoln, London, St. Albans, Tadcaster, Winchester, York—grew up and developed.

It must not be thought that all these Roman towns have had a continuous and unbroken history since the time of their foundation. That is not the case. When the Roman legions withdrew from Britain, most of their towns were deserted and fell into decay. For example, we know that Chester was deserted for more than three centuries, and Silchester (once a very large Roman town, situated at a most important centre of communications) was never reoccupied and is today only a village. Even London was deserted for several decades. Indeed, of all the towns founded by the Romans, only Exeter and Winchester certainly, and Lincoln probably, can boast a continuous history through the centuries.

In a sense, with these towns of Roman origin, it is not the town itself that is important, but the name. It will be noticed that many of those I have mentioned end in "chester," which is the Latin *castra*. This termination always implies an original encampment on a highway. Thus from the name we can deduce much of the town's history.

And it is the same with Saxon and Danish towns. Actually, we know very little indeed of the Saxon towns. Whereas the Romans were essentially an urban people and strongly attracted to a communal life, the Saxons were essentially an agricultural people for whom towns held little attraction. They borrowed from the Romans, especially in the way of material from the buildings which the Romans had left, and they sometimes built on the ruins of Roman towns, though it would seem that in no case did they follow the Roman town-plan. Quite apart from this, as might perhaps be expected from an agricultural people, they were not very good builders. We have left a few examples of Saxon work in some churches, but nothing whatsoever of Saxon domestic architecture has survived. And of Danish architecture in this country nothing at all remains. But, as with the Romans, the place-names live on and provide a certain indication of the town's origin. The Saxon terminations are *ton*, *ham*, and *burgh* (borough): the Danish or Scandinavian terminations are *thorpe* and *by*.

But, though we know nothing of the appearance of Saxon towns and though it is true to say that the Saxons were not an urban people, yet it is to the Saxons that we owe the foundations upon which our present system of local government is built. It was the Anglo-Saxon King Edgar who instituted the holding of a law court within the burgh, a court presided over by the port-reeve and composed of

THE CATHEDRAL OF ELY

the burgesses or, as we would call them today, the aldermen. These courts were held three times a year (though there were usually a number of smaller additional meetings) and from them have come our present town councils and quarter sessions. The Normans took over this system and greatly enlarged it, granting many charters of incorporation and so laying the foundations of our modern municipal system.

The Normans were also architects and builders of a very high order. They are best known, of course, as builders of great castle-fortresses. It must not be forgotten that for many years after the Conquest, the Normans were but a small minority living in the midst of a largely hostile population. Their castles had, therefore, to be strong and had to be placed in strategic and dominating situations. Ample evidence of this is to be seen time and again in England today. In place after place, we find the castle occupying the best position with the town huddled on the slopes and in the valley beneath it. In all such cases (and many are post-Norman: the great era of castle-building in England was in Plantagenet times) it may be taken that the castle was built for some particular purpose—the guarding of a frontier, or a river crossing or some other important line of communication—and that the town grew up afterwards. Charming examples of this are to be seen at Durham, Arundel, Knaresborough, Guildford, Lewes, Nottingham, Windsor and Richmond (Yorkshire). And I suppose that it is largely for this reason that we have so few hill-top towns in England. Indeed, there are perhaps only two that can truly be called hill-top towns; Bishop's Castle and Shaftesbury.

Shaftesbury, perched on a hill commanding enormous views over the surrounding countryside, grew up around a Benedictine monastery and is an outstanding example of the many English towns that owe their origin to some monastic foundation. It would be impossible to over-stress our debt to the monasteries. Long before the towns grew up around them, the monasteries had built schools and hospitals and homes for aged folk, had made gardens and established drainage systems. Some of the schools, some of the hospitals, some of the homes for old people may still be seen in towns up and down the country. But, more important even than this, the monasteries gave us a tradition of building and of order which we have never lost. Many of our cathedral cities—and they are among the most beautiful of our towns—are monastic in origin. Notable examples are Canterbury, Norwich, Bristol (one of the most exciting towns in England), Oxford, Ely, Peterborough, Worcester, Gloucester and Chester.

Unlike the Roman towns, which were usually square with two main highways crossing in the middle (examples of this plan may still be seen in many of our towns, but perhaps the best of all is Chichester where the two main roads meet in the centre of the city at one of the most magnificent crosses in England), the medieval town had no set plan. Originally, nearly all of them grew up along

NOTTINGHAM—THE CITY HALL AND MARKET PLACE

"THE most handsome city centre of England." This is a description often given to the old market place with the modern city hall, pictured above. Nottingham's market has been transferred to a nearby covered "hall" and the square has been transformed into attractive gardens. The famous Nottingham Goose Fair was formerly held in the square in the first week of October but this too has now been transferred to another site. The city centre was re-designed between 1920 and 1930, while the city hall was completed in 1929. Many of the houses surrounding the square, however, are much older dwellings and retain the projecting upper storeys supported on pillars which used to be a feature of this part of the city. Among Nottingham's other famous buildings are the castle, rebuilt in the seventeenth century and now used as a museum and art gallery, and the modern University buildings.

each side of a main thoroughfare. They were towns with length but no breadth. Only if there was a cathedral with its cloisters, or if the town was so situated as to be a commercial centre (when there would be a market-place which was usually square), was there any breadth. As trade increased, as the countryside became better farmed, the demand for markets naturally increased and where there was no market square the main street was, in some cases, widened to make room for traders' stalls. Sometimes these streets attained an astonishing breadth. Outstanding examples of this commercial enterprise are to be seen at Marlborough, Baldock, Dunstable, Bedale, Bridgnorth, Thame and High Wycombe. Beyond this, however, there was no town planning. If one did not know anything about architecture or history, one would still be able to place correctly in time the majority of English medieval cities simply by the multitude of winding lanes.

The next great influence, greater perhaps even than that of the monasteries, came with the sudden increase of traffic in the eighteenth century. Transport, which had hitherto been both difficult and uncomfortable, became in a few short years comparatively easy. The great number of stage coaches produced a steadily increasing number of travellers in all walks of life, and an enormous demand for over-night accommodation. It is to the age of the stage coach that we owe some of the finest inns in England. There were, of course, inns in England long before the stage coach, but these had mostly been the hospitals run by the monasteries or hostels run by some benevolent Lord of the Manor (good examples are *The George* at Glastonbury and the *New Inn* at Gloucester), but these and their like were quite unable to meet the demands of the stage coach. And so inns were specially built. Ipswich, Dunstable, Stamford and Chelmsford possess particularly good examples of the coaching inn.

And the coaching inn brought in its train the stately town house. These wonderful examples of dignified Georgian architecture may often be found hard by the coaching inn, for the simple reason that their owners thus had much less difficulty in catching the coach. Perhaps the best example of this juxtaposition is to be seen in Broad Street, Ludlow. This simple, but very dignified, architecture, though with a few embellishments (for this was the age of taste), stretched on into the Regency period. But now it was coupled with the most careful and skilful town planning. The spas of the nineteenth century—especially Bath and Cheltenham—and the seaside resorts (notably Brighton), which became all the rage at about the same time, are wonderful examples of this.

The Industrial Revolution of the nineteenth century had a tremendous effect both on the appearance and the development of our towns, a greater effect than any other single factor in our history. No one now bothered about space, and expense became an all-important consideration. The aim was to get workers sited as near as possible to the factories in which they worked. The result was miles and miles of uniformly poor houses, grouped together anyhow, without plan and certainly without beauty. Yet as these industrial towns grew and became entities, they developed a strong civic pride of their own. Some of the finest civic buildings in England are to be found in the industrial towns of the north—in Rochdale, Huddersfield, Bradford, Halifax—and the finest civic centre in England and Wales is that at Cardiff.

At the same time, it must not be forgotten that we owe the beauty of many of our towns to the Industrial Revolution. These are the towns which were by-passed by the railways, left in quiet solitude with the architecture of a previous and more gentle age. Chipping Campden is the one that leaps to mind, but there are, of course, many others.

With all these widely different factors playing their part in a country which, for almost one thousand years, has been free from invasion, there is naturally a great diversity in our towns. We speak of Cathedral Cities and Market Towns and so on. But it is not really possible to make so clear a distinction. Yet, it is true that there are no two towns alike in appearance in England—and it is no less true that the towns of a district or region have a family likeness. No one can mistake the family likeness between Chipping Campden and Witney. No one can mistake the black-and-white of the west midlands, the tile-and-brick of south-eastern England, the flint of East Anglia, the stone-and-slate of the north. And this is due, of course, to the use of local building materials.

One of the saddest things about new building in this mid-twentieth century is the frequency with which local material is discarded in favour of some foreign material. One of the saddest things about modern development in towns is the uniform architecture with uniform paintwork which is now appearing everywhere in connexion with the buildings of some of the multiple stores. The beauty of England's towns is very largely due to the lack of uniformity in style, and this is now in great danger of disappearing. In fact, attention has been so concentrated on the preservation of the countryside that the towns have been neglected and are now in every whit as great a danger.

It is only by getting to know them in the bustle of day and in the still of night, by studying their situation and realizing its purpose, by knowing the wealth stored up in their names and in the names of their streets, that we come to value them for what they are: not the least part of our heritage and infinitely worth preserving.

Brian KnoxFitzGerald

BOSTON STUMP

BOSTON "Stump," a landmark over the fens of Lincolnshire, is the Gothic tower of the parish church of St. Botolph. The tower, with its imposing octagonal lanthorn, is almost three hundred feet high and dominates the market square on one side and the River Witham, which hereabouts is tidal and reveals a wide expanse of mud at low water, on the other.

North Country

FOR nearly 1,500 of the last 2,000 years the towns of North-east England were outposts—bulwarks against aggression from across the border. Two factors made this inevitable, first their geographical position and second the wealth and fertility of the land between the Pennine Chain and the North Sea.

From the end of the first century A.D. Hadrian's Wall, a great chain of fortifications linking the mouth of the Tyne with the Solway Firth, formed the effective boundary of the province. To the north the land was held by the Picts and the Scots, the latter being tribes who came originally from Ireland, the former the descendants of the Iron Age people and of still earlier civilizations. To the south there were all the accoutrements of Roman provincial government, fortified stations, well-protected settlements and the walled towns which were the basis of the civilization of Roman Britain.

York was one of the most important of these latter; indeed it was one of the three or four most important walled towns in Roman Britain. Throughout the occupation Roman legionaries were stationed at York, which thus began its long history as a garrison town.

York once more became a sizable town and most of the towns and villages of today also began to take shape. Then there were the alarms and terrors of invasion again as the Norsemen from Denmark and Norway did precisely what the Saxons had done hundreds of years before, landing on the east coast, devastating the towns and making new settlements. Some towns such as Whitby show by their very names that they were Viking foundations (most of the towns and villages founded by the Norsemen have names ending in "by" or "thorpe"). It looked at one time as though the whole of England would come under the sway of the Vikings. The north-east did in fact form part of the empire of the Danelaw after the Treaty of Wedmore.

The Vikings or Danes (the two names are interchangeable) developed some of the historic towns in this area as centres of administration and fortified strongholds. These "Danish boroughs" included Lincoln, Derby and Stamford, as well as the Midland towns of Nottingham and Leicester.

The Danish Peace, as it was called, did not long rest on the north country. By the middle of the tenth century all the towns of the north were once more in English hands, though many of the Viking colonists were allowed to remain. This was especially true in the Viking settlements along the east coast of Yorkshire, which was virtually inaccessible from the mainland.

When the Normans came to England William the Conqueror saw the weakness of his position in the north country as also in the west, and ordered the fortification of many of the towns in strategic positions. So great castles were raised in York and Newcastle, Richmond, Berwick and Carlisle and many other places. Unlike the Midlands, which were guarded with few castles, the north country literally bristled with these massive fortified homes.

Farther to the south and rather removed from the centres of border warfare, towns like Beverley and Ripon flourished in an ecclesiastical atmosphere, for at both the chief power resided in the Church and the monastic order concerned was the chief landowner. This was even more true of Durham, which still looks half castle, half cathedral town.

There is no other Durham in Britain, just as there is no other York and no other Lincoln and no other Chester. These four cities alone make the north country proud of its historic towns.

Compared with the broad expanse of the Vale of York and the pleasant undulating country of Northumberland, the north-western quarter of England has little of nature's wealth in the fertility of its soil. Far more mountainous than the north-east, it has not a single navigable river north of the Ribble and only one great traffic artery, the classic approach from England to Scotland through Kendal and Carlisle. For the rest, there are the steep forbidding Pennine moors to the east and the frowning massif of the Cumbrian Mountains to the west.

Farther south, the narrow plain broadens out into the new lands of Lancashire, where modern industry has changed the face of the countryside beyond all recognition.

All these factors determine the background of the few historic towns in north-western England. There is Carlisle, a place of importance from the earliest times because it commands the route into Scotland. There is Lancaster guarding another vital point on the same route and like Carlisle for many centuries a fortified town and vital strategic point.

Just as the Cheshire Plain strikes a new note in scenery and tradition, so Chester, its centre in history and in commerce alike, is also completely different from any of the other towns of the north-west. This is a city with a long historic heritage starting in Roman times, justly proud of its ancient history, and of its medieval buildings and still, like York, a walled town.

The industrial revolution has been remarkably uneven in its incidence on the north-west towns. All have grown, but the three most historic cities, Chester, Lancaster and Carlisle, have grown, one feels, according to plan, whereas the towns of the cotton belt from Manchester to Burnley, from Oldham to Blackburn seem to have sprung up overnight, undisciplined and now scarcely capable of being reduced to order.

THE CITY OF DURHAM

MEDIEVAL cathedral stronghold, modern industrial and commercial centre, the city of Durham is built on a steeply rising hill half encircled by the River Wear. At a distance Durham still has very much the air of a medieval city, with its massive three-towered cathedral and prominent castle rock. From Norman times onwards the castle was the stronghold of the bishops, who held special privileges from the Conqueror and were charged with the defence of the north-eastern counties as well as with the organization of the episcopal see. The Bishop of Durham, who in the reign of William the Conqueror was created Earl of Northumberland, held powers comparable only with those of the Bishop of Ely and was virtually a ruler in his own right independently of the Crown. Durham Cathedral remains one of the finest examples of Norman architecture in the country. Its nave rests on massive Norman piers, the whole style of architecture being more severe and more durable than corresponding examples in the south of England. What remains of the castle has been incorporated in the building which now houses part of the University of Durham which was originally founded in 1646 by Oliver Cromwell, but was dissolved after the Restoration of King Charles. It was refounded by Act of Parliament.

NEWCASTLE-ON-TYNE

EXCEPT in the restricted area by the water front, modern Newcastle shows few signs of its historic past. It is a spacious, busy town with a growing population of well over a quarter of a million, the undisputed commercial centre of one of Britain's richest coalfields and a port in its own right with a still extensive trade, especially in coal—a fact which was the origin of the phrase "coals to Newcastle." The River Tyne is crossed by the high level bridge on the left, which carries road and railway and was built in the middle of the last century, by the swing bridge, from which this photograph was taken, and by a recently built bridge farther downstream which has the longest single arch of any bridge in Britain. Among the many towers and spires which are a feature of every view of modern Newcastle, the two-hundred-feet-high Gothic tower seen here behind the castle stands out. This is the tower of the former parish church of St. Nicholas, which attained cathedral status in 1882. The square battlemented building in the foreground is the twelfth-century Norman keep of the castle which gave Newcastle its name. The walls of this great keep, which have an average thickness of about fifteen feet, have withstood the ravages of nearly eight hundred years and still show few signs of decay, in spite of the corroding effect of the smoke pall which often darkens Newcastle's sky. Near the castle, on the right, are seen the Georgian-style pillars of the Guildhall. The story of Newcastle begins much earlier than the foundation of its castle, for there was a Roman station here associated with the point farthest downstream at which the Tyne could be crossed and from which Hadrian's Wall started.

FORTRESS TOWNS OF NORTHUMBERLAND

BAMBURGH (*right*) and Alnwick (*below*) are two of the most ancient strongholds of the north-east coast. Bamburgh was the capital of the Anglo-Saxon kingdom of Bernicia; Alnwick, as the principal residence of the Earls and Dukes of Northumberland, became the very centre of government in the north-eastern counties during the later Middle Ages. No big town grew up round Bamburgh—today there is only a quiet village a hundred yards or so from the basalt rock on which the castle is built. The town of Alnwick, however, grew to be one of the largest towns of Northumberland and is still a busy market town and tourist centre. Both castles are still inhabited. The Norman keep of Bamburgh is the only surviving part of the early stronghold. Alnwick retains more of its medieval battlements which date mainly from the fourteenth century. But these, too, unfortunately have been over-restored.

INSIDE CARLISLE CATHEDRAL

THIS is the choir and east window of Carlisle Cathedral, once the priory church of an Austin foundation and a church of an episcopal see since early in the twelfth century. Most of the nave of what was considered the most glorious ecclesiastical building in the north was destroyed during the great civil war so that only a fragment survives today, making Carlisle a relatively small, though architecturally distinguished, cathedral. Its crowning glory is the great east window, shown here, which includes some fine medieval stained glass and is a most splendidly conceived example of Decorated Gothic tracery.

BERWICK-ON-TWEED

THIS ancient town, which was a cockpit of fighting during the Border wars, preserves to a remarkable degree the atmosphere of coaching days. Berwick is the Border town *par excellence*; mainly on the Scottish bank of the river it is properly described as an English town and is included for administrative purposes in Northumberland, yet its own county, Berwickshire, is a county of Scotland. Said to have been taken by storm fourteen times, Berwick finally became English and was established (and remains) as a "buffer" state.

YORK MINSTER AND BOOTHAM BAR

THE county town of Yorkshire, yet independently of a status equal to that of the three Ridings, the ecclesiastical centre of the north of England, ranking second only to Canterbury in English Christendom, and a vigorous modern industrial and commercial centre, York is unique in combining a thriving economy with many links with every period of its storied past. The circuit of its ancient walls is almost complete (apart from the section which was never walled because of the protection offered by riverside marshes) and several of its gates (or "bars") are well preserved. That shown (*above*) in close proximity to the Minster is Bootham Bar. The Minster was founded at least as early as the seventh century, the first wooden chapel being attributed to St. Paulinus, one of the original band of godly men organized by St. Augustine in Canterbury. By the time of the Norman occupation, York was already leading religious thought in the North. By the end of the eleventh century a new church had been built on the site; this with frequent alteration and enlargement forms the basis of the present Minster, which is the largest cathedral church of the old foundation in Britain. Almost the entire architecture of the Minster is Gothic (only the groundwork and lower parts of the walls being Norman), the latest additions are the graceful towers which were constructed during the latter part of the fifteenth century.

SCENES IN ANCIENT YORK

MUCH of York's commerce until the middle of the nineteenth century was centred on its river, on which craft of many kinds still ply for business and pleasure. Much of the riverside is lined with warehouses or by contrast with walks and gardens but, as the photograph (*above*) shows, there are still a number of handsome Georgian buildings reflecting the time when the river bulked largest in the town's prosperity. Some of the streets in the very centre of the city have survived the clearance that was carried out in the last century. Among these the Shambles (*right*) is the quaintest and most remarkably preserved. This was the street of the butchers (whence its name) at a time when individual trades were invariably congregated in a single district. The almost perfect stretch of the city walls (*below*), largely but most faithfully restored, is a link with the thirteenth and fourteenth centuries, when the town was often threatened in the Scottish Border wars.

RICHMOND, YORKSHIRE

THE name "Richmond" derives from Norman-French and means "Rich Mount." The castle (*above*), built by the Normans, became Henry VII's favourite residence in the North and he named his palace at Sheen after it. From that derives the present Surrey borough of Richmond. The older part of the northern city is full of cobbled streets, such as that at Carnforth Bar (*below*), and some of the houses date from the sixteenth century.

GREYFRIARS TOWER

THE Gothic tower (*above*) is the only substantial fragment remaining of the church of the Grey Friars which was built towards the end of the fifteenth century when wealthy citizens of Richmond endowed the friary for the rebuilding of its church in the magnificent style of the times.

22

THE MARKET SQUARE AT RIPON

THERE is much in common between Ripon and Beverley. Both are centred on large hand-some market squares, both have a famous church, and both are thriving centres of rich agricultural land. Ripon cathedral is in origin even older than Beverley Minster. A bishop was appointed to the see before the end of the seventh century, but the bishopric lasted only a few years. After that the Minster was the church of an abbey and did not attain cathedral status again until 1836. The market place has many famous old buildings, including the Wakeman's House, which from the thirteenth century onwards was the residence of the Wakeman or Mayor who blew the traditional "horn" at nine o'clock as a curfew.

23

ANCIENT CITY OF CHESHIRE

CHESTER derives its name from the Roman word "castra" meaning "camp." Throughout almost the entire period of the Roman occupation of Britain it was a garrison town. The walls, though not so extensive as those of York, are just as intact and, as at Canterbury and many other ancient towns, follow closely the line of the Roman walls. Here (*left*) is a part of the wall with the Phoenix tower, one of the medieval battlements, alternatively known as King Charles's tower because it was here that in 1645 King Charles I watched the battle on nearby Rowton Moor. There are many ancient houses in Chester, including the famous Rows (*below*) half-timbered houses above a covered arcade including shops.

CHESTER CATHEDRAL

THE glory of Chester is its cathedral, a noble building of red sandstone which includes almost every style of medieval architecture from Norman to Tudor. Chester was recorded as a place of worship in the seventh century. This view is of the choir looking west towards the great Gothic west window and shows the section of the choir stalls which include in the misericords some of the finest fourteenth-century medieval wood-carving in Britain.

COUNTY TOWN OF LANCASHIRE

LANCASTER is a far more ancient place than the majority of towns in Lancashire's industrial belt. Moreover it is situated towards the north of the county away from the more populous centres of cotton manufacturing and marketing. The result is that though it has grown widely since the industrial revolution it has preserved to a much greater extent than the others its nineteenth-century appearance, and apart from its relatively small industrial quarter is well planned and laid out. In the general view of the town (shown *below*) some older cottages and houses, including a beautiful Georgian-type residence, are close to the ancient castle. The keep of the latter is shown (*left*) floodlit. The site of the castle is of a Roman station, from which Lancaster derives its name.

ENGLAND'S GREATEST FISHING PORT

GRIMSBY, at the mouth of the Humber on the Lincolnshire shore, is sometimes described as one of the greatest fishing ports in the world. The number of trawlers and drifters which operate from its docks is approaching a thousand. Yet little more than one hundred years ago this was a small coastal village with an insignificant trade by sea and small local fisheries. The turning point in its history was the building of the modern docks between 1850 and the end of the century. These made Grimsby one of the best equipped ports on the east coast and attracted extensive shipping trade with the Continent in addition to encouraging the expansion of the fishing industry. In the picture (*below*) fish freshly landed is being packed into aluminium boxes for carriage by road or rail to the inland towns of England. Of the total population of Grimsby, approximately 100,000, it is estimated that nearly half are engaged in the work of the port and the fishing industry. On the right is the 300-foot-high hydraulic tower which dominates the port area.

A NARROW STREET IN LINCOLN

LINCOLN is one of the most interesting of England's historic towns. As at Durham, the ancient settlement was on a hill protected from attack by a steep cliff-like decline falling to the River Witham. On that hill most of modern Lincoln's links with its past are situated, though the town has spread out along the river and on its farther bank. It is at the river level that most of its industries and more recent housing estates are situated, in close proximity to the docks, which still handle a sizable river traffic. The old hill town which was medieval Lincoln, including the cathedral and the castle, is uncommonly resistant to the encroachment of modern "development." There are many old cobbled thoroughfares like the one pictured on the left with half-timbered or brick-built houses having plaster fronts and the architecture of two or three hundred years ago.

THE EXCHANGE GATE AND THE CATHEDRAL

THIS is the very centre of ancient Lincoln—a broad cobbled square backed by the entrance to the castle and looking toward the fourteenth-century Exchange Gate, the main entrance to the cathedral close, with the three towers of the cathedral behind. In the foreground, left, are two contrasting styles of the town architecture of bygone ages, the steep-pitched gables and overhanging upper storeys of the half-timbered Jacobean style and the four-square classical frontage of late Georgian and early Victorian days. Many of the old houses in Lincoln around the cathedral were built in Elizabethan days or earlier; when later the city was reconstructed their owners had new frontages built in conformity with the style of their own day, while leaving the interior virtually untouched. So it happens that many of Lincoln's dwelling places have classical Georgian fronts but timbered Jacobean or Tudor living-rooms. There is, too, in Lincoln, only a stone's throw from the cathedral close, one of the very earliest domestic buildings still extant in Britain, the Jew's House, a stone dwelling place with round-headed Norman windows which must have been built not later than the twelfth century. Lincoln, too, is the only English town which retains a Roman road gate (the Balkerne Gate at Colchester is merely a postern). The castle was one of the first Norman fortresses and was completed according to the records within five years of the landing of William of Normandy. The ruins surviving include a late Norman keep. The cathedral is without dispute the finest feature of Lincoln today, as it has been for nearly nine hundred years. Of the three towers, the central is the earliest while the two west towers, nearest the camera, are the best examples in Britain of the Decorated Gothic style.

LICHFIELD—THE TRIPLE SPIRES OF THE CATHEDRAL

A QUIET oasis in the middle of a crowded town, the cathedral of Lichfield with its three spires known as "The Ladies of the Vale" is on the site of a cathedral which like Lincoln and Dorchester was once the see of the Saxon bishopric of Mercia. St. Chat in the seventh century was one of its earliest bishops. More recently the city has become known as the birthplace of Dr. Samuel Johnson, hero of James Boswell's immortal biography. The name Lichfield is said to mean "the Field of the Corpses." Today, as always, the importance of the city of Lichfield is as a market town in a region predominantly agricultural.

Midland England

MIDLAND ENGLAND is the quietest countryside of all Britain. It is an area of charming landscapes, of low hills and rolling downs, but it also includes part of the dead level of the Fens and impinges in the north and west on the uplands which lead ultimately to the Pennine Chain and the Welsh border hills.

The historic towns reflect the moods of the landscape and its varied story. In the extreme eastern marches of the Midlands, Huntingdon and St. Ives, which stand on the very threshold of the Fens, inevitably draw much of their historic interest from their proximity to the natural boundary of East Anglia. Ely's story is unique but it is the story of an outpost of civilization in the midst of the uninhabited Fens rather than that of a city of the mainland. For hundreds of years the Isle of Ely was a world of its own over which the Bishops of Ely wielded very nearly absolute power. Because of its position, hemmed in by the marshes on every side, Ely won fame in medieval times as the home of lost causes, the refuge of Hereward the Wake and of many other Saxons.

A feeling of peace broods over many of the east midland towns which have not been afflicted by the blight of nineteenth- and twentieth-century industrialization. Oakham, for instance, the capital of England's smallest county, Rutland, has a castle, it is true, but a castle which was never designed for warfare but was built late in the Norman period primarily as a residence at least a hundred years before its time. The castles of other Midland towns seem less massive and warlike-looking than those of most areas. This is partly because the majority were built in the county towns and today are half lost in a welter of modern buildings.

Before the Norman conquest the Midlands formed the least prosperous part of Saxon England. Most of it fell within the province of Mercia, which was always a kind of buffer state between Northumbria and Wessex, never as strong as either of them except in the time of King Offa, who built the great dyke against the Welsh. Later, when the common enemy was the Viking invader and England was partitioned, the Midlands lay between the area which was indisputably Norse and the settled Saxon kingdom to the south and south-west.

When King Alfred made peace with the Norse invaders, part of what is now Midland England fell within the Danelaw, that part of the realm which was given over to the Norsemen to colonize as a price for a period of comparative peace. Nottingham and Leicester, for instance, were Danish boroughs, while

31

most of what is now Northamptonshire came under the foreign yoke. Then within a few generations the Saxons were fighting back over this disputed territory and the midland towns had to be resettled again. The result was that by the time of the Norman occupation they had little tradition behind them and quickly took on the characteristics of Norman market settlements. It was as market towns, therefore, that most of them developed.

Today there is a sharp contrast, more clear-cut than in any other part of England except west Yorkshire, between the old towns which have remained county and market centres and those which have been overwhelmed by the industrial revolution. The Midlands have coal—that is a fact more important to the present than any historic heritage. When England began to be an industrial country it was found more economic to bring raw materials to the coalfields than to transport the coal to the traditional centres of medieval industry. That is the true origin of the Birmingham complex and of the Black Country.

Most of the industrial towns have a long history, even though it is forgotten in the swift expansion of the last 150 years. Birmingham was mentioned in the Norman Domesday Book, while in the sixteenth century it was a manufacturing centre for cutlery and tools as well as a flourishing market town. How important it was to the nation's industry in the seventeenth century is shown by the fact that it was one of the chief arsenals of the Roundheads though its "big guns" were mostly swords. It was nearly the end of the seventeenth century before Birmingham's first actual gun was made.

How different are the old market towns only a relatively few miles away. Stratford-upon-Avon and Warwick are happily as ancient in appearance as they are in history. In the midst of the hunting shires there are quiet towns like Market Harborough and Uppingham. Even Lichfield, which in its own way is a busy industrial town with more than a little of the midland grime, is still first and foremost a cathedral city and a place of historic memories.

Midland England in the broadest sense of the term has two cities which embody the traditions of medieval learning. Oxford and Cambridge are very different, for they represent respectively the heritage of southern England and that of eastern England but they have in common the ageless beauty of mellow buildings and the unchanging spirit of places which for five hundred years have held aloft the torch of scholarship—and still do so in a changing world. Both are cities, though Cambridge has only attained that dignity in recent years, but whereas Oxford is a medieval stronghold town, Cambridge remains essentially an overgrown village or market town. There is nothing in Cambridge quite so devastating as the notice outside the station which has greeted so many thousands of visitors to Oxford by train, "This is Oxford where Morris cars are made."

STAMFORD—THE MAIN STREET

STAMFORD is one of the several attractive stone-built Midland towns along the Great
North Road. It owed its early importance to its position as market centre for the rich
lowland area on the borders of the Fens; it attained a new prosperity in the eighteenth
century through the large number of visitors it entertained as a stopping place on the main
coaching highway from north to south. Stamford, like Grantham and the others, has several
coaching inns, one or two of them transformed into modern hotels. Its graceful main
street is dominated by the tower and spire of the church of St. Mary. Its name is a link
with the troubled times of the ninth and tenth centuries, when for a few decades it was one
of the chief towns of the Norse or Danish province, formed after the Treaty of Wedmore.

MORE OF WARWICK'S OLD BUILDINGS

HERE (*above, left*) is the Eastgate and the church of St. Mary, which was rebuilt after the Reformation and (*above, right*) some fine timbered houses with the Westgate and the tower of St. James's Chapel in the distance. *Below* is a view of Warwick Castle, which according to tradition is on the site of a Saxon palace of Queen Ethelfleda and for many centuries has been the seat of the Earls of Warwick, whose family has played a very prominent part in shaping the history of England especially during the reign of King Edward IV.

IN OLD WARWICK

STILL the county town of its shire, Warwick is far older than Birmingham. The latter has become a vast industrial and commercial complex; Warwick has resisted the changes consequent on the industrial revolution and remains a country market town. Half-timbered houses, some Tudor, some Jacobean, and nearly all built from timber hewn when the forest of Arden was still an important source of building material, line the main street.

COVENTRY

THOUGH Coventry was very severely damaged in the much publicized German air attack of the Second World War, some parts of the old city survived. One such corner shown (*right*) is the courtyard of Ford's Hospital. The cathedral was almost entirely destroyed but the remaining ruins (*centre*) are being preserved and incorporated in the layout of

the new cathedral. A photograph of the architect's model reproduced at the foot of the page shows clearly how this is being done.

"RIDE A COCK HORSE TO BANBURY CROSS"

"Ride a cock horse to Banbury Cross" says the old nursery rhyme, though whether an ancient market cross or merely the crossroads is referred to is not at all clear. Banbury Cross today, pictured here, is at the junction of the roads from the North and Midlands, but it has no claim to antiquity. When it was set up in 1858 the nursery rhyme was already hallowed in tradition. Yet it is a handsome example of Victorian craftsmanship and includes among the figures around the base a fine likeness of the Queen herself. Banbury's other claim to "legendary" fame is as the place at which Banbury cakes were first made. The trim row of houses and shops seen in the right background dates from the early part of the nineteenth century when Banbury drew prosperity from the heavy coach traffic. Banbury remains an important market town with a number of very flourishing light industries.

STRATFORD-UPON-AVON

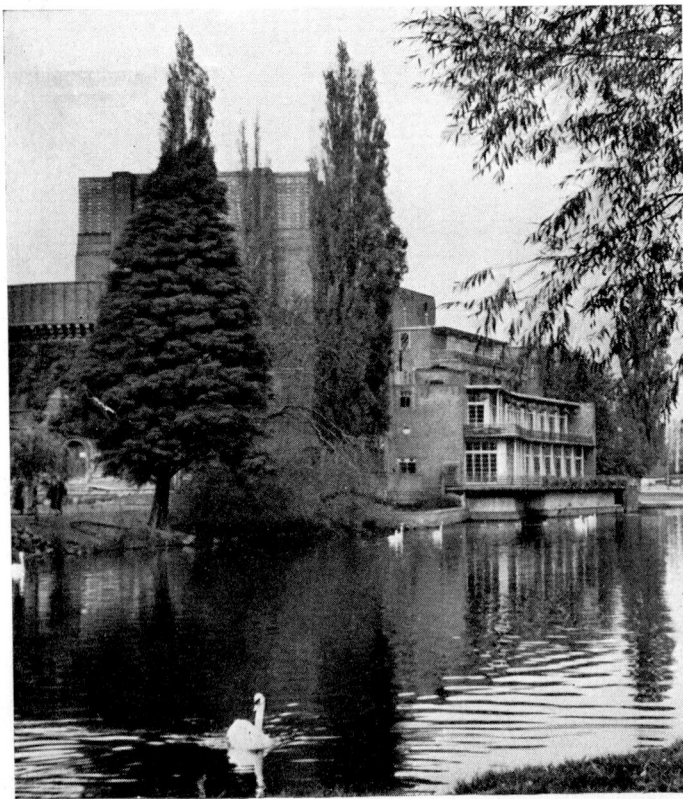

STRATFORD is best known as the birthplace of William Shakespeare. In fact the accident of the "Bard of Avon's" birth has altered the whole history of this little town. Literally hundreds of thousands of visitors come every year, drawn by the town's associations with England's greatest poet and dramatist. Apart from Shakespeare's birthplace there is New Place, where he lived during his last years; the Church of Holy Trinity, which contains his tomb; and, above all, the Shakespeare Memorial, including the modern theatre (pictured *left*) completed in 1932 to take the place of an earlier structure that was destroyed by fire. The picture of the High Street (*above*) shows the Garrick Inn and Harvard House on the left.

38

CITY OF DREAMING SPIRES

OXFORD, cathedral city, university town, and more recently important industrial centre, is unique in the number of medieval buildings it possesses and in its atmosphere of age-old quietude, blended with the hurry and bustle of a modern town. The High Street (*above*) and the Corn Market are thronged with shoppers and country visitors, while fifty yards away the narrow twisting lanes of the medieval city are almost untouched by time. There are traditions of the foundation of a university by King Alfred the Great, who by tradition is reputed to be the founder of University College silhouetted in the left foreground of the photograph. Before the Reformation Oxford was well established as a centre of learning, but it was the interest which Cardinal Wolsey showed in Oxford at the time of the dissolution of the monasteries that gave it a pre-eminent place in the whole world of learning. Since Tudor days many new colleges have been added and older ones have been enlarged. That is how it happens that Oxford as a whole is an incomparable storehouse of the architectural styles of every period, from Gothic to the nineteenth century and the present day. The cathedral was at one time the church of a nunnery which dated from the eighth century and dedicated to St. Frideswide, who was one of the earliest friends of the university.

TOM TOWER

TOM TOWER (*below*) is the gateway of Christchurch College, known as "The House." Christchurch is pre-eminently Wolsey's college and the Tudor kitchens and hall are still extant. The tower was added later to the design of Sir Christopher Wren. It derives its name from the bell, Great Tom, which still tolls 101 times just after nine o'clock, the original curfew hour of the college, the number of strokes being the number of members of the original foundation. The gateway leads into Tom Quad, largest of the quadrangles.

MAGDALEN TOWER

MAGDALEN TOWER is the first sight of the university city which greets travellers approaching from London by the bridge over the River Cherwell. It is a late fifteenth-century tower, one of the loveliest in Britain, beautifully situated between the "High" and the river. It has won additional fame as the scene of the Mayday celebration when a choir sings hymns in Latin at sunrise. This photograph is taken from the Botanic Gardens which are said to have been laid out in 1623 and are thus the oldest of their kind in Great Britain.

40

OXFORD: THE WAR MEMORIAL

ABINGDON ON THE THAMES

ABINGDON, one of the oldest towns in Berkshire, has had a separate existence since early Saxon days. Its medieval importance derived from its abbey, which was founded before the end of the seventh century and re-endowed soon after the conquest, thereafter becoming a powerful and wealthy foundation around which a small market town grew up. *Above* is a general view of the town from the boathouses, showing some of the handsome riverside dwellings and the noble spire of the parish church, a landmark for miles over the level pasture lands of the surrounding countryside. *Left* is a closer view of the market square with on the right the Renaissance market house which superseded a market in the square.

42

GATEWAY TO THE COTSWOLDS

SUCH is the familiar description of Burford, Oxfordshire's graceful stone-built town on a hill sloping down to the River Windrush at the eastern end of the Cotswold plateau. *Below* is shown the fine sweep of the main street looking north towards the river and the low hills which rise from its farther bank. The stone-built, stone-roofed houses of sixteenth or seventeenth century origin blend perfectly with the newer dwelling places farther down. Many of the latter also are built of the locally-quarried oolitic limestone.

THE ROAD TO THE CHURCH

THE quiet road (*above*) leads off Burford's main street and ends at the church which is hard by the river's bank. Sometimes known as the cathedral of the Cotswold, Burford parish church is a splendid example of architecture at the end of the great Gothic period of church building. Its tapering spire is unusual but the perpendicular tracery of the windows, one of which can be seen in the photograph, is characteristic of all the great Cotswold "wool churches."

43

CITY OF LEICESTER

LEICESTER is the perfect example of an ancient town which to the casual observer shows no sign of its antiquity. Its continued importance through the ages is due to its position at the meeting place of main lines of communication and its proximity to the River Soar, which for centuries was an important additional means of transport. The story of Leicester began during the Roman occupation when under the name of Ratae it was one of the largest and most flourishing of the provincial centres of the Roman province, a place excellently served by several new roads constructed by the Romans. Early in the Saxon regime it achieved fresh importance as the see of one of the bishoprics of Mercia. Later still it was in Norse occupation and one of the towns which the Viking invaders turned into "boroughs." The city's modern industrial importance is based on the manufacture of footwear and hosiery, of which it has become by far the most important centre. Today Leicester has more than a quarter of a million inhabitants and continually increases.

A VILLAGE CAPITAL

OAKHAM is the administrative centre and county town of England's smallest county, Rutland. Though it has modern shopping thoroughfares and an increasing number of summer visitors, its ancient square around the church and market cross (shown *right*), with the castle only a short distance away, still looks rather like a country village. The market cross is known as the Butter Cross, and is a reminder of the rich agricultural area of which Oakham is the geographical centre. Under the Butter Cross are the ancient stocks.

IN OAKHAM CASTLE

OAKHAM CASTLE is a manorial residence built late in the Norman period when the risk of armed rebellion by the Saxons had receded. Most of the Norman building has disappeared but the banqueting hall with beautifully-carved pillars (shown *left*) is intact. It is used now as a museum which contains the finest collection of horseshoes in the world, composed mainly of the shoes presented according to a medieval custom by every peer of the realm and every member of the sovereign's family who visit the town.

45

OLD TOWNS OF HUNTINGDON

HUNTINGDON (*above*), and St. Ives (*below*) has each in its own way played an important part in moulding the history of England. Each stands athwart the River Ouse as it approaches the dead level of the fens. Each has had a modest prosperity from the earliest times, deriving from its position as a market centre. Huntingdon's fame was enhanced by Oliver Cromwell, who was baptized in the former church of St. John and educated at the Grammar School, living later at the house now known as Cromwell House. Cromwell lived at St. Ives also for a number of years. St. Ives' greatest claim to antiquity is its name, which may refer to St. Ivo, a legendary saint who helped in the conversion of Saxon England. The stone bridge, from which the photograph (*below*) was taken, is a more certain link with ancient times, as is the chantry chapel on the bridge, seen clearly on the left.

NEWARK-UPON-TRENT

THOUGH always known as Newark-upon-Trent, the river which flows past the ruins of Newark's famous castle is in fact the Devon, a tributary of the Trent, into which it flows a mile farther downstream. Newark's history through the ages has had two facets, the events connected with the castle (shown *below*) and the more peaceful life of commerce and trade which has always been centred, as it is today, on the market square (*right*) which is dominated by the lofty tower and spire of the parish church. Newark lies on the Great North Road, which by-passes the centre of the town but crosses the bridge beside the castle ruins. On this road, apart from the castle, there is little to remind the traveller of Newark's historic heritage. By contrast, the market square is surrounded by graceful old houses, by the classical pillars and ornaments of Georgian times when Newark was a regular stopping place for many of the hundreds of stage coaches and private carriages which passed through it on the journey from London to York and Scotland. The castle, of which such substantial ruins stand today, was originally a palace-castle belonging to the Bishops of Lincoln and ascribed to the same Bishop Alexander who was responsible for rebuilding part of Lincoln cathedral. The main gateway of the castle (extreme left background of the photograph) dates from this first palace; most of the rest belongs to a later restoration. The last years of the castle as a residence were in the great Civil War, when Newark was a staunch stronghold of the King and its castle was besieged for many months by the Roundhead troops. Finally, like so many others, it was dismantled by order of Oliver Cromwell the Protector. Newark has given its name to a special plaster for the manufacture of which it has for a long time been a centre.

DERBY: ST. ALKMUND'S CHURCHYARD

MIDLANDS CONTRASTS

PETERBOROUGH and Derby have in common a progressive industry and a prosperous commercial life which started at the time of the industrial revolution and have increased without greatly altering the character of either town. Each is the traditional centre of its county, in the case of Peterborough, the Soke, which is virtually a county within a county (Northamptonshire). There the resemblance ends. The pride of Peterborough is its cathedral (*right*), a truly magnificent Norman foundation. It retains its Norman character, especially the west front, though the elaborate arcading pictured here is of later date. Derby has a cathedral, too, the Church of All Saints, one of the churches elevated to the status of cathedral in the period between the two wars. The photograph (*below*) shows St. Mary's Bridge over the River Derwent, with the lofty spire of St. Alkmund's Church and the nineteenth-century tower of the Roman Catholic Church of St. Mary in the background.

THE CITY OF CAMBRIDGE

CAMBRIDGE has only recently been granted the status of a city. Yet through the industrial development of the last 150 years Cambridge has preserved far better than Oxford the quiet and cloistered atmosphere of a city of learning. Until the turn of the century, when motor-cars and omnibuses transformed its streets, it was justifiable to describe it as a "village." Even today its centre is little changed, its market place and narrow streets surrounding it quite unsuitable for the volume of traffic. In essence Cambridge still consists of three converging roads, which unite and cross the main bridge over the Cam by Magdalene College. The photograph on the right shows Trinity Street the most westerly and the one nearest to the river, from which it is divided only by a line of colleges running from St. John's to Peterhouse.

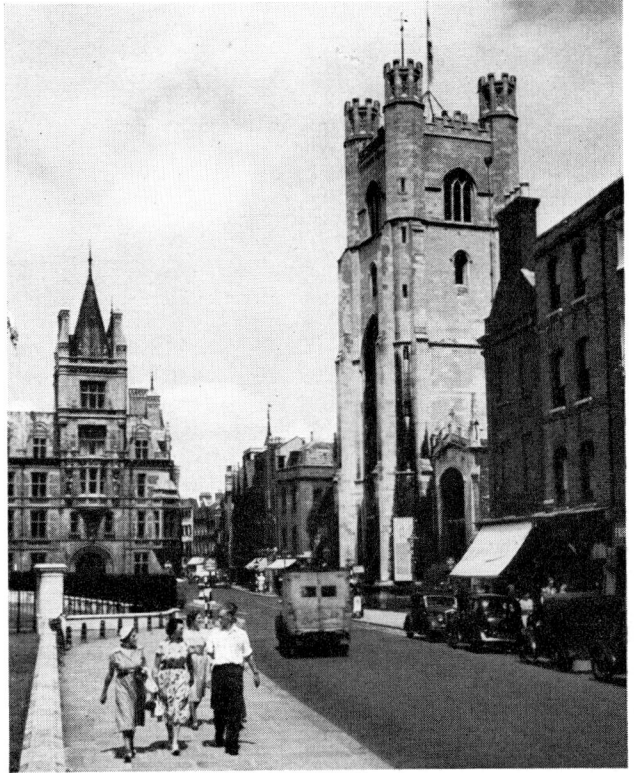

KING'S COLLEGE AND ITS FAMOUS CHAPEL

ALTHOUGH by no means the oldest college in the university, King's is one of the most handsome as well as one of the most famous, while its chapel (*opposite*) may justly claim to be one of the finest monuments to fifteenth-century architecture in the whole of Britain. The noble perpendicular lines of the window tracery and of the buttresses, and the sculptural quality of the main entrance arch are well shown. King's College was founded by Henry VI, who also founded Eton College. The chapel was started within a few years of the foundation but was not completed until well into the reign of Henry VII. That explains why the Tudor rose is such a prominent feature of its detail. Another outstanding feature of the chapel is the number of late medieval stained glass windows. These were added after the main building was completed and date mainly from the decade 1520 to 1530. By the time of the foundation of King's there were already a number of separate colleges in existence. Both Clare College and Trinity Hall were founded during the first half of the fourteenth century, so were Gonville and Caius (pronounced Keyes) and Corpus Christi, and probably also Pembroke and one or two others. The oldest by tradition is Peterhouse, of which there are records before the end of the thirteenth century and which appears then as a foundation under the patronage of the Bishops of Ely. The university was important enough by 1318 to win the recognition of the Pope in Rome. According to one poorly authenticated story, the university was founded by dissidents from Oxford. Certainly before it became a centre of learning Cambridge was a small and unimportant place founded on virgin ground during the later Anglo-Saxon period. It was known first as Granta's Town, named after the River Granta. Much later its name became corrupted into Cantebrigge and as the fame of the town exceeded that of the river, the river itself became known as the Can or Cam and so eventually the name of Cambridge itself became established.

CHURCH LANE, LEDBURY

The West Country

THE West Country has developed a tradition which is peculiarly its own but corresponds in a way with the warlike tradition of the north. For hundreds of years while modern Britain was taking shape the whole area—a broad wedge from Cheshire southward to Monmouthshire and Gloucestershire—was a no-man's-land, strife-ridden in the long struggle between England and Wales.

There have been many boundaries between England and Wales. The dividing line is still a nominal one, which though it looks definite enough on the map as a division between the counties of England and those of Wales, bears little relation to racial or national strains. Monmouth, for instance, which is for administrative purposes an English county has deep-rooted Welsh traditions and contains some of the richest of the Welsh coalfields and some places such as Ebbw Vale— villages that have become industrial towns—which without reference to a map even now most people would unhesitatingly attribute to Wales. So it is in lesser degree all the way up the boundary. Montgomery is in Wales, Bishop's Castle is in England, Overton is in Wales, Ellesmere in England. It is always so where two countries are divided by no well-marked physical feature and by no clearly defined racial distinction.

Historically the division has been between the lowlands of England and the highlands of Wales. Offa's Dyke, that great earthwork of Saxon days which most probably marks the civil division between the lands of Mercia and those of the Welsh princes, follows a more logical line than the present boundary. It is a safe assumption that if it were possible to redraw the map even today with no vested interests to consider the result would be quite different from that shown in a current atlas.

Such factors are the determining ones in the story of the historic towns of the West Country. Cheshire in the Middle Ages was a county palatine, with some-thing approaching self-government under its Earls: the Fitz Hamons at Gloucester had almost royal prerogatives, the Earls of Shrewsbury and Hereford were at times virtually independent of the Crown. The fact that they did not more often rebel against their king was due not so much to their own lack of ability as to the fact that their rear was always unprotected. In Monmouth and Hereford and Shropshire they left behind them traditions of cruelty and oppression which lingered for many centuries and soured the temper of the country people who lived on the borders of Wales. One can attribute to the ruthlessness of the Marcher

Earls the once strong anti-English feeling of the people of Radnor and Montgomery, who in spite of coming within the sphere of English authority hundreds of years before there was legal union between the two countries are often today more national in outlook than the folk of the mountains or of the more distant counties of the south-west.

Sometimes fighting on a big scale flared up between the English and the Welsh, especially during the reign of Edward III. In these struggles of the Middle Ages Monmouthshire was a special cockpit of fighting since it commanded the royal road from England into the Vale of Glamorgan and towards the "Little England beyond Wales" which is Pembrokeshire. To the Welsh people the line of the Severn always appeared a more desirable boundary than the many proposed by successive English kings. Fighting swayed first one way then the other, and frequently extended as far as the crossings over the Severn specially round Gloucester, which was not free from the fear of attack until Tudor times.

The great strength of some of the castles in this part of the country is testimony to those troubled times. The castle of Newport where the Wye joins the Severn and where the medieval road to the west forded the Wye still stands impressive though in ruins and remains the dominant feature of this old town that has been an outpost of England since Norman times. The fortresses of Caerphilly and Cardiff are in Wales now but belong to the same chain of castles and are even stronger. Monmouth commanded an important road ford over the Monnow, Hereford one over the Wye, while Shrewsbury was responsible for the protection of the upper Vale of Severn where it broadens out into a plain after emerging from the Welsh mountains. Worcester and Gloucester gave a second line of defence.

We can divide most towns of the West Country into these two categories— the forward springboards of attack and the bases in the rear. There is a third division which consists of the ancient towns which lie farther to the east towards the Midlands. These grew up in comparative peace and security confident in the sure bulwark of the Severn and in the strong fortress towns which lay between them and the Welsh. Several of them were not walled towns in the Middle Ages, nor did they have a castle to protect them. They were rather market towns, the life and soul of the Cotswold country and of the rich agricultural areas in the eastern half of Worcestershire and Shropshire.

Evesham, Chipping Campden and Cirencester stand out from a number of others. The modern story of Evesham with its near neighbour Pershore depends on the orchards which are such a beautiful feature of the countryside around and now extend out of the vale towards the foothills of the Cotswold around Chipping Campden. The story of Chipping Campden, Cirencester and the other Cotswold market towns is in the past rather than the present and is wrapped up in the story of Britain's medieval woollen industry.

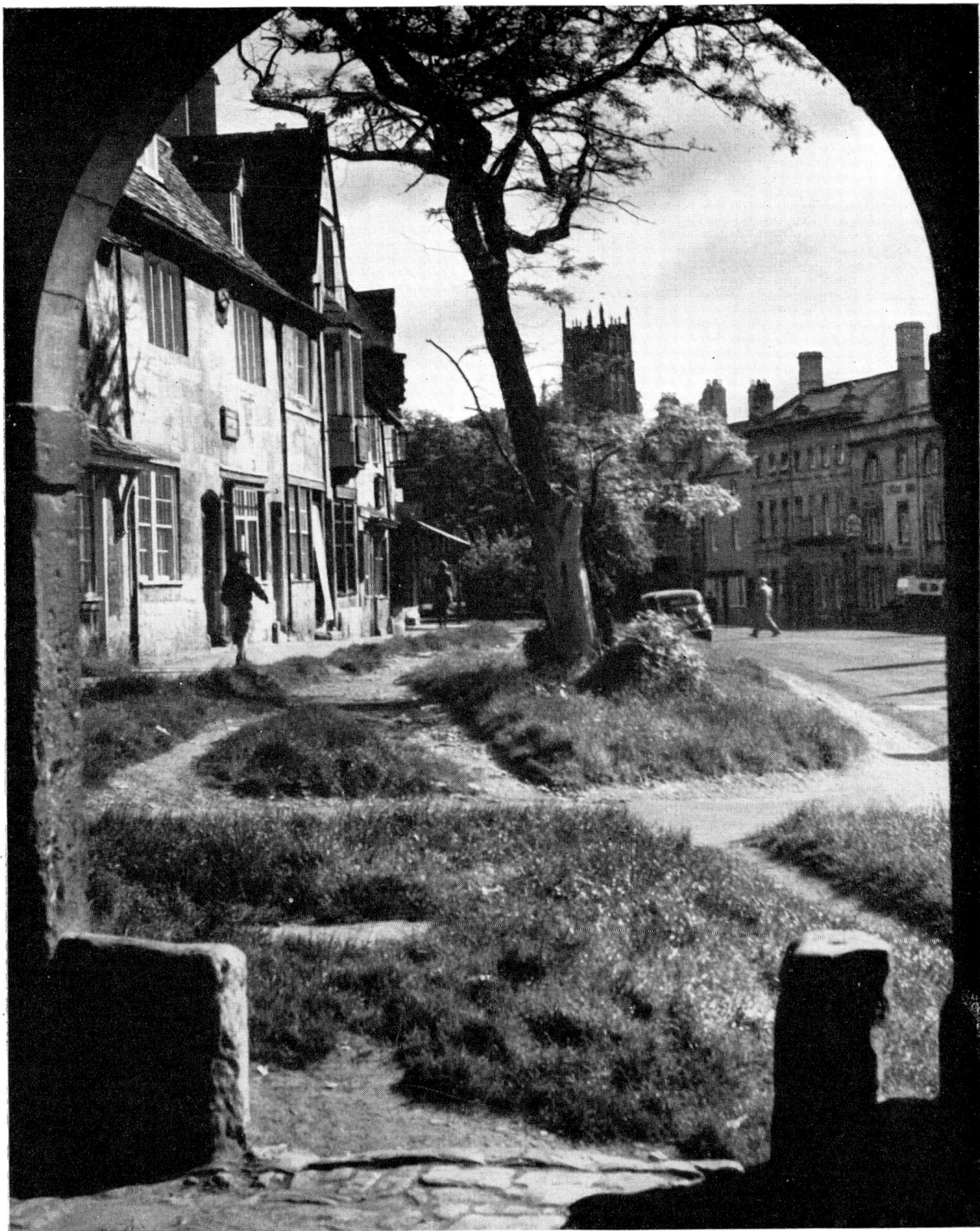

CHIPPING CAMPDEN—THE HIGH STREET FROM THE MARKET HALL

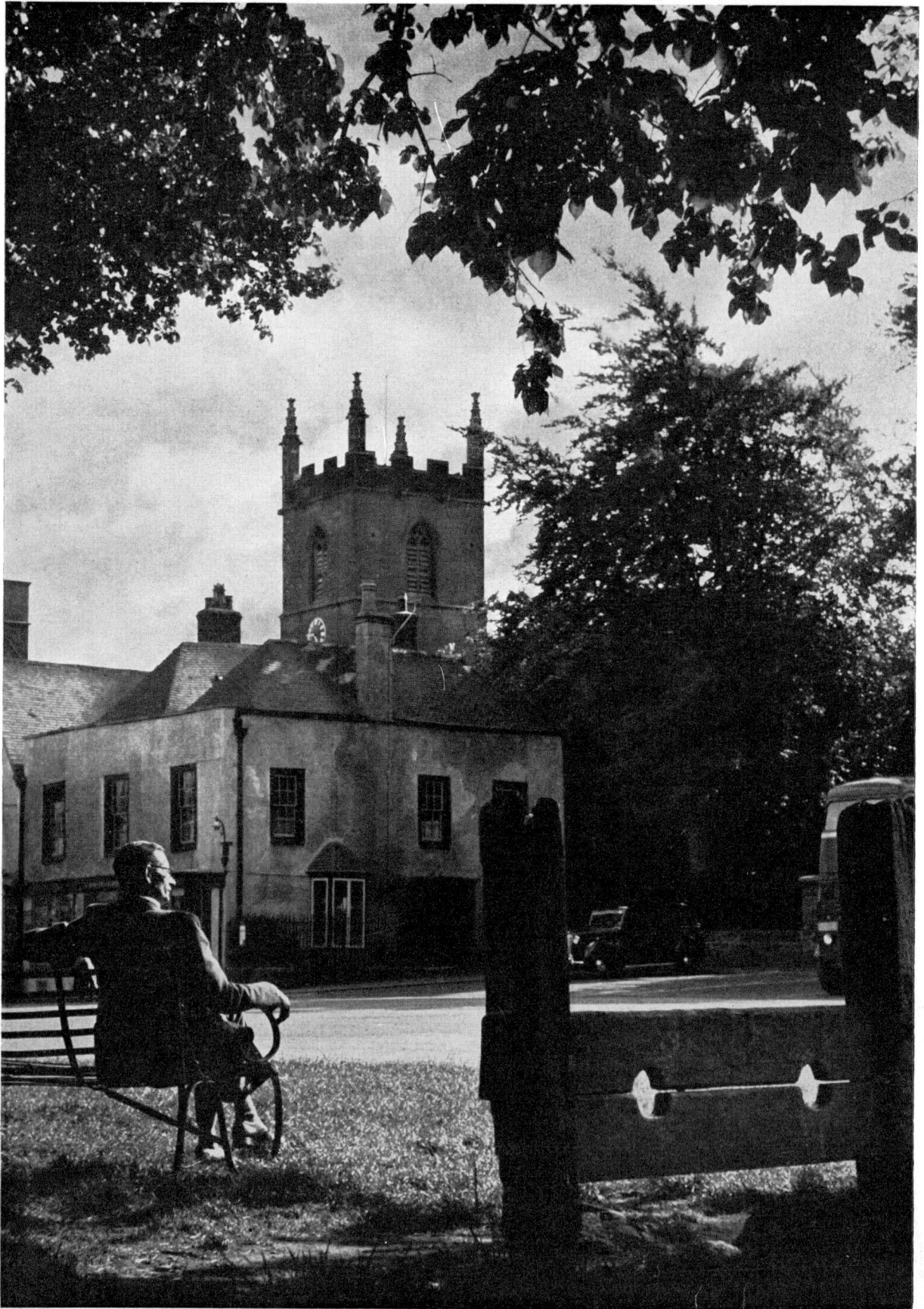

COTSWOLD TOWNS—I

ON the right is an unusual view of Cirencester in Gloucestershire one of the chief towns of the southern part of the Wold. It is also the most ancient of the Cotswold towns, for it dates back to Roman times, when it was known as Corinium, and was an important market and transport centre on the great Fosse Way which linked the south-western districts of the Roman province with the Midlands and the North. Through the Middle Ages, which were especially prosperous in this part of England (see below) and up to the present time, Cirencester has remained a market town of importance. The pride of Cirencester is its church and the crowning glory of the church is its magnificent Gothic tower, a landmark over hundreds of square miles of the rolling Cotswold countryside.

COTSWOLD TOWNS—II

STOW-ON-THE-WOLD (*opposite*) is one of the chief towns of the central Wold, though it has never achieved the size and importance of Cirencester; since the building of the railways its growth has been retarded by its position high-set on a hill with the nearest railway station some distance away in the valley. So it happens that Stow still consists chiefly of its wide square surrounded by graceful houses varying in date from the sixteenth to the nineteenth century and a few little roads which radiate from the square. Its "village green," too, is intact, with the ancient stocks which look across the broad street to the square-towered church, itself a handsome building though less elaborate than those of Cirencester or Northleach. The story of these Cotswold towns has much in common, for they were all founded before the Norman conquest but remained relatively small and insignificant until Britain's medieval woollen boom began. The fourteenth and fifteenth centuries were their heyday, for the Cotswold country proved ideally suited to the rearing of sheep and Britain's greatest wealth was in the marketing and manufacture of wool. At first it was the raw material for the weaving industry of the Low Countries that was in greatest demand. Then the prosperity of the Cotswold farms was still modest and the wealthy merchant class was only just beginning to emerge. Later when most English wool was manufactured into textiles in the weaving shops of local towns the farmers grew wealthier but their new-found wealth was exceeded by that of the merchants and manufacturers. These two wealthy classes used much of their surplus in the enrichment of the town churches, many of which were rebuilt or enlarged or had new towers added to them. The farmhouses, too, were rebuilt in the attractive local stone and showed the way to the development of the Tudor manor house, while the merchants built for themselves magnificent dwelling places, such as those in Broadway and Chipping Campden.

COTSWOLD TOWNS—III

MORETON-IN-THE-MARSH is pictured in both the photographs on this page. It is yet another of the pleasant stone-built towns in the Wold country. As its name suggests, it lies in a long fertile valley between ridges of the Wold and has shared in the best of both worlds—the prosperity deriving from the rich sheep pastures in the Middle Ages and the substantial wealth which came later to most English country towns in country suitable for mixed farming. Among its many old buildings are the White Hart, just on the left of the photograph below, where Charles I and Henrietta Maria are said to have stayed during the Civil War, and the market house (in the centre of the picture) a less ornate counterpart of the market hall of Chipping Campden. Moreton's main street (*left*) is lined with trees with here and there a grass verge gay with daffodils in spring, making a charming frontage for the old stone-built houses. Moreton continues to be a thriving market town.

EVESHAM shares in the half-timbered style of ancient building common in the Western Marches (*left*).

ANCIENT EVESHAM

EVESHAM'S position at a natural crossing of the Avon ensured its early development but its growth in the last two hundred years has occurred chiefly through its position as the market centre of the Vale of Evesham, one of the richest agricultural areas in the west, and the main fruit-growing area of Britain apart from Kent. The town grew up, like so many other medieval towns, round its powerful Benedictine abbey, which was founded in the eighth century and re-endowed after the accession of William of Normandy. The isolated tower (*right*) is the chief link today with this ancient abbey, a belfry tower built only a few years before the dissolution of the monastery. In the abbey the great Simon de Montfort was buried.

59

ANCIENT CAPITAL OF SHROPSHIRE

SHREWSBURY is one of the stronghold towns which grew up round castles first built in Norman times to protect the Western Marches of England against the wild and warlike Welsh tribes. Long before that it was a settlement which is named in connexion with the pre-Roman Celtic civilization. The castle was rebuilt again and again, the last time at the end of the eighteenth century. It is still in use as local government offices. The picture (*left*) shows one of the many seventeenth-century streets with its beautiful half-timbered houses in the true tradition of Marcher architecture. The street's name is Grope Lane. *Below* is the main bridge spanning the Severn, an ancient bridge formerly known as English Bridge. It was remodelled between the two world wars. In the background is the noble spire of St. Mary's Church.

SCENES IN OLD HEREFORD

HEREFORD is another of the historic towns of the Marcher country which were the cockpit of fighting during the long struggle between the English and the Welsh in the Middle Ages. As at Shrewsbury, there was a castle here which was more than once besieged by Welsh insurgents; not a trace remains of it. Only the name is preserved in Castle Green. The castle itself was dismantled at the close of the Civil Wars. The picture (*above*) shows the road bridge over the River Wye leading into Bridge Street, with the tower of the cathedral on the right. The cathedral is on the site of a Saxon foundation and was the see of a bishopric by the eighth century. Even in those early days Hereford was the target of attacks by the Welsh and it is recorded that the cathedral church was utterly destroyed during one such raid just before the Norman occupation. The rebuilding carried out during the first century of Norman rule is the basis of the present cathedral, which is one of the most attractive and less massive large churches in the Norman style. The impressive square tower is one of the latest parts of the church dating from the first half of the fourteenth century. Among the cathedral's many treasures are the medieval Mappa Mundi and the chained library (*below, right*) of the sixteenth century. Among the old houses of Hereford is the Jacobean town house (*below, left*) beautifully restored and furnished in accordance with the period of its construction and known today as the Old House.

GLOUCESTER, THE CATHEDRAL CLOSE

GLOUCESTER, like Cirencester, was an important Roman town on the extensive network of communications established over the West Country during the Roman occupation of Britain. Its name then was Glevum. The modern town, a busy market and industrial centre as well as a cathedral city is dominated by the fine fifteenth-century tower of the cathedral (*left*) which is more than two hundred feet high and one of the most elaborate of its kind in the whole country. Around the cathedral are grouped a number of pleasant Georgian houses and some of older foundation with a lower storey of stone and an upper one half-timbered.

GLOUCESTER, THE NEW INN

ONE of the oldest buildings in the modern city of Gloucester is the New Inn. "New" in this context means some time in the fifteenth century; it was built to relieve the pressure on the monastic lodgings when many pilgrims were coming each year to the cathedral. The pleasant galleried courtyard (shown *right*) recalls that three hundred years later the New Inn, rebuilt and enlarged, won fame as a hostelry for travellers who were journeying by stage coach towards South Wales.

CHELTENHAM, GLOUCESTERSHIRE

CHELTENHAM, the famous spa of the West Country, lies seven miles north-east of the city of Gloucester. It is a well laid out town of wide and handsome streets, many dating from the first half of the nineteenth century. Those shown on this page are (*above*) a corner of Montpelier Walk, constructed between 1826 and 1830 to the design of J. B. Papworth; (*below, left*) Royal Crescent, which was built in 1810-12, and (*below, right*) Lypiatt Terrace.

THE RIVER SEVERN AND THE BRIDGE AT

WORCESTER WITH THE CATHEDRAL BEHIND

TEWKESBURY, GLOUCESTERSHIRE

TEWKESBURY is yet another of the medieval towns which grew up round its abbey. After the dissolution the abbey church became the parish church and remains an exceptionally beautiful Norman building. Its square massive tower can be seen in the picture. Tewkesbury Abbey was one of the earliest of the large Norman foundations, most of the present church being completed before the middle of the twelfth century. In recent times Tewkesbury has become a city of literary as well as historic pilgrimage through its associations with the novel *John Halifax, Gentleman*. It has a large number of fine half-timbered houses in the typical Welsh Marcher style, some of which are seen in the riverside view below.

THE TOWN AND CASTLE OF CHEPSTOW

CHEPSTOW is the most southerly of the border fortress towns guarding the valley of the Severn and its more important tributaries. The castle is situated on a steep bluff rising from the broad stream of the Wye at the point where it has always been forded by the coastal road from Gloucester to South Wales. It is thus a point of special strategic importance which was guarded not only by the strong castle but also by town walls acting as a second line of defence. The town came into existence under the protection of the castle on the steep slope of the hill which falls to the Wye. The gateway (right) is one of the original medieval gateways of the town. The picture above shows the castle rock and the substantial ruins of the mainly fourteenth-century structure, an Edwardian rebuilding of a castle dating from the eleventh century. The Norman keep was converted to a banqueting hall.

67

WELSH FORTRESS TOWN

LUDLOW in the Middle Ages was one of the chain of fortress towns held against the Welsh. A castle was built on the cliff rising above the River Teme before the end of the eleventh century. Of this early building the Norman keep survives. In later reigns the castle was enlarged and strengthened and was a residence of the Earls Marcher and their successors, the Lords President of the Marches. The view below shows the great extent of the castle ruins. The bridge is the medieval one over the Teme which is so narrow that large vehicles cannot pass, yet it carries most of the heavy traffic between Shrewsbury and Gloucester. In the town itself (*left*) there is a pleasant mixture of Elizabethan, Georgian and modern architecture. Here the Georgian market house looks across the narrow street to one of the half-timbered houses.

THE COUNTY TOWN OF MONMOUTHSHIRE

MONMOUTH, like the other ancient towns pictured in this section, has a story closely interwoven with that of the struggle between England and the Welsh chieftains of the Middle Ages. It lies at an important strategic point near the entrance to the Wye gorge where the River Monnow flows into the Wye. To this historic background there is added the bustling activity of a modern county town and agricultural centre and a history in more recent times which has more than usual interest. Of the castle little save the foundations survive but the site has a special interest as the birthplace of King Henry V, known to history as Harry of Monmouth from this accident of birth. His statue appears in the photograph (*above*) in a niche of the wall of the Shire Hall, a typical building of the first half of the eighteenth century, when Monmouth's expanding trade and the settled conditions of its fertile countryside inspired the citizens to raise a building worthy of the town's prestige. In the cobbled square in front of the hall there is the statue of another Monmouth man who brought fame to the town in a very different way many hundreds of years later. That was the Honourable Charles Rolls, who was the first man to fly the English Channel in both directions. *Below* is one of Monmouth's links with the Middle Ages, the thirteenth-century bridge gate at the crossing over the Monnow. This is one of the earliest town gates in such an intact condition in all Britain and the only bridge gate of its kind which has survived. Nearby is the Beaufort Arms, another of the large and famous coaching inns, and here Lord Nelson stayed with Lady Hamilton.

69

TRURO, THE RIVER AND THE CATHEDRAL

South-west England

THE south-west is the Celtic England of tradition, inhabited before the Norman conquest by the same tribes which formed the basis of the population of Wales. Devon and Cornwall were in fact in the seventh century a part of the kingdom of Wales. When the two were divided Devon and Cornwall continued to be known as West Wales.

The Saxons never exercised much influence beyond Exeter. The same is true of the Normans, although they had a castle at Launceston which became the outpost of government in the west. So it continued all through the Middle Ages, the people of Devon and Cornwall going their own way, observing their own customs and maintaining a genuine independence of thought and conduct even though they were formally incorporated in the realm. Somerset and Dorset formed the border country between Saxon and Celtic England, though Dorset at least was always more Saxon than Celtic.

Exeter today is the administrative and market centre of the whole of Devonshire. When Roman Britain was declining Exeter beat off many a Saxon raid but was never utterly destroyed as were the Roman towns of eastern England. Then with the Norman occupation it took on new importance as a Norman outpost against the always recalcitrant Celtic population to the west, becoming "English" enough as the centuries passed so that Queen Elizabeth thought it proper to bestow on it the motto of "*Semper fidelis*" (always faithful).

By then Devonshire had become famous for its seafaring traditions. Exeter shared in these as a port, linked with the sea before the end of the sixteenth century by a ship canal which was the earliest of its kind in Britain. Because of its wonderful position on lines of communication, it has never looked back.

The same is unfortunately not true of many of the famous old ports of Devon and Cornwall which had almost equal fame and prosperity in the sixteenth century. Barnstaple and Bideford, St. Ives and Looe, Kingsbridge and Padstow, to name only a few at random, were large and flourishing places when the sailing ship was the easiest form of communication and before transport by railway or road had been dreamt of. All these, of course, still have a real commercial importance but their glory lies in the past, whereas the pride of Exeter is as much of today as it is of yesteryear. The medieval fairs of Barnstaple and Kingsbridge are still celebrated with many of their legendary customs. At both a stuffed glove decked out with a garland of flowers is hung from the council house during the fair as a token of welcome to the thousands of visitors who flock into the town from the countryside. Yet one is left with the feeling that the annual fair has lost a good deal of its economic significance; its accent has changed to pageantry and the "fun of the fair."

What strikes the visitor most of all is that few of these old ports have extended far beyond their medieval limits. Yet all of them are still ports, some of them like Barnstaple with wharves which deal with cargoes from overseas.

Until there were railways there was little traffic in the south-west except by sea, any more than there is today between the coastal towns of Norway. When the railway was driven through Exeter to Plymouth and Penzance and later opened up every part of both counties, the demand for the slower ships was lessened. When the steamship supplanted the sailing vessel, the greater draught of the new vessels made many of the old ports unsuitable to receive their cargoes. The tale, of local calamity but national benefit, was completed when motor lorries began to transport goods from door to door, from farmhouse to the markets of London, from factory to port, and even from one coastal town to another.

Through all this the most historic port of the south-west continued to flourish. In Plymouth's case, with its position on the shores of perfect natural anchorage, the coming of steamships enhanced its prestige and ensured its continuance as a great port. There is a wonderful consistency about Plymouth's story which is co-extensive with the story of the fleet. Today the Navy represents probably the largest single profession of Plymouth and the neighbouring towns.

Beside the romance of the far south-west the historic towns of Dorset and Somerset might strike some as rather drab. They are far from that; though perhaps they lack something of the character which has made the seaports of Devon and Cornwall what they are. Two at least of Somerset's famous towns have a unique history. The first of these is Glastonbury, which is the sole link in southern England between the Christianity that was introduced during the Roman occupation and the new religious feeling which came to life in the later days of Saxon England. Like Bury in Suffolk, Glastonbury owed its all to the monastery which was the very centre of its life and the essence of its being. Whether or not St. Joseph of Arimathea founded the first church on its site as legend relates, the fact remains that the abbey of Glastonbury was certainly established before the missionary Augustine came from Rome to the Court of Kent.

The story of Bath is very different but none the less striking. This is a city which has three times risen to heights of fame and wealth, the first time when it was one of the chief spas of the Roman world, the second when the abbey of Bath was a rich and vigorous foundation, and the third when Beau Nash made it the centre of Georgian fashion. The growth of industry on its outskirts in recent years has given it the chance of a fourth heyday.

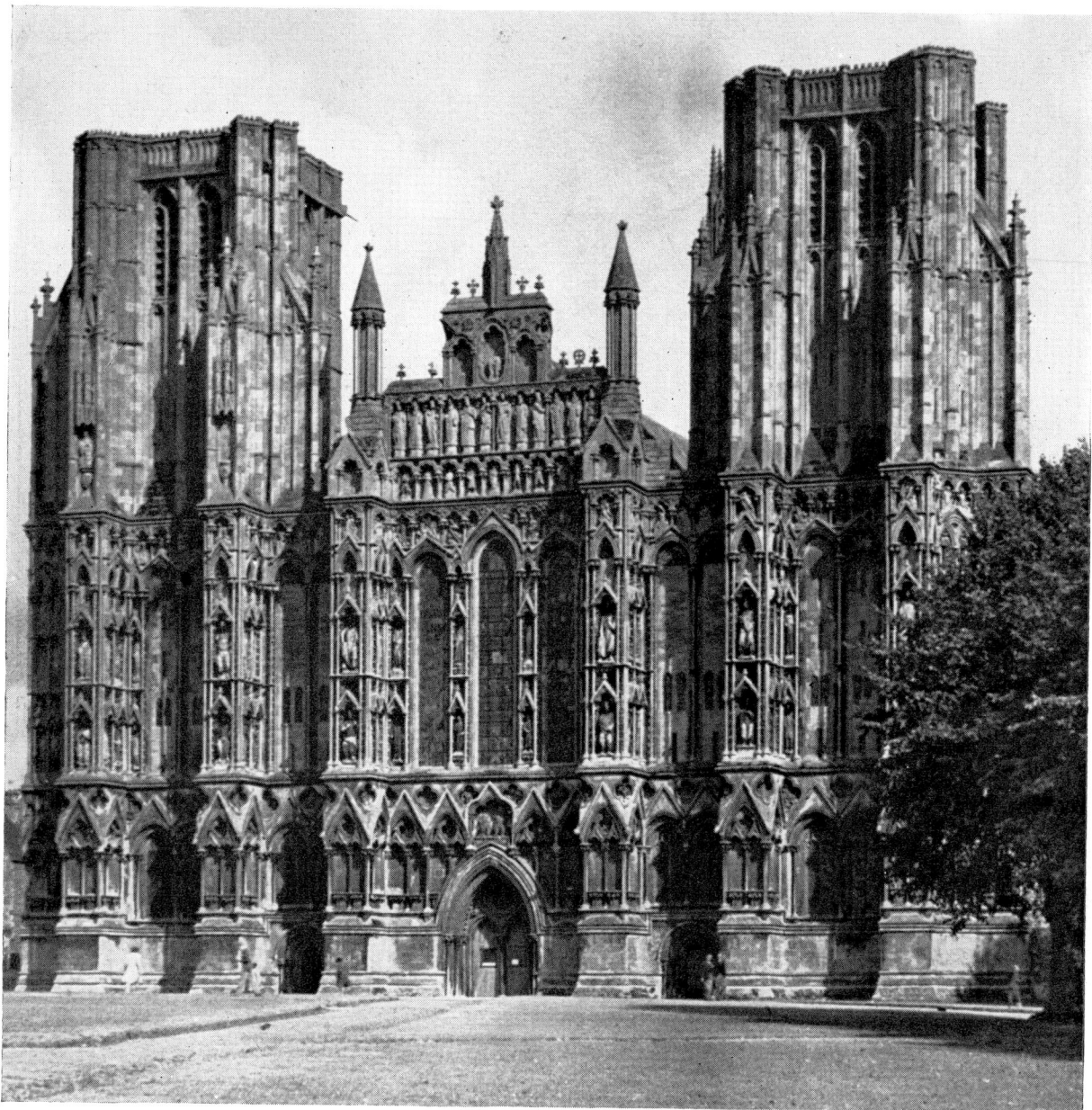

WELLS CATHEDRAL, THE WEST FRONT

THERE was a bishopric at Wells 150 years before the Norman occupation, though only for a comparatively short time. Later the see was transferred to Bath Abbey and not restored to Wells until the thirteenth century. Thereafter the bishopric was named after both cities, and the bishop is known to this day as the Bishop of Bath and Wells. The greater part of the cathedral dates from the thirteenth century; it was consecrated in 1239. The west front is generally said to be the finest example of the Early English phase of Gothic architecture in the country. The arcading is unique, the 350 statues contemporary with the fabric represent Old and New Testament kings and bishops, angels and prophets, with set pieces depicting the Coronation of the Virgin and Resurrection of the Dead.

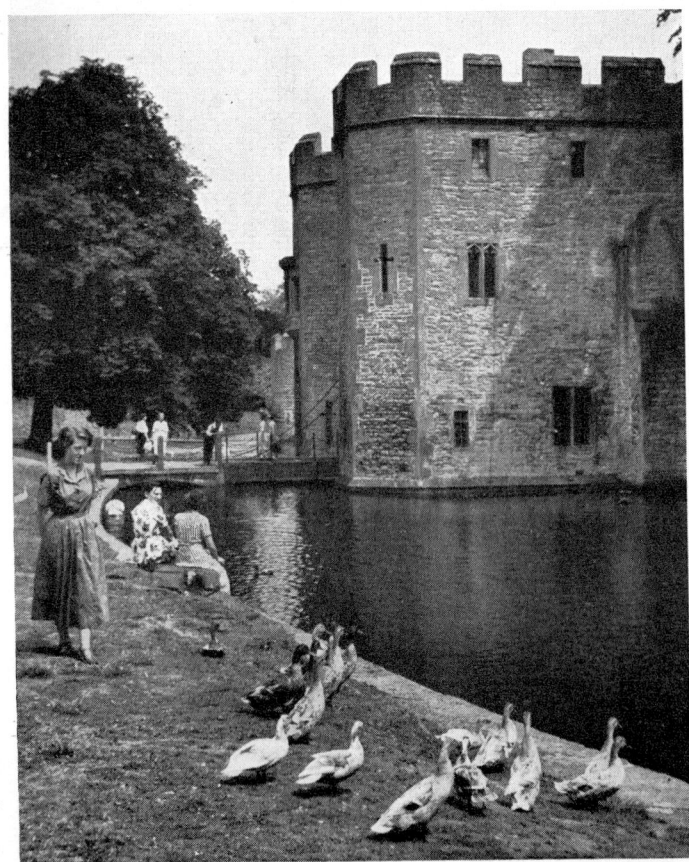

IN THE OLD TOWN OF WELLS

WELLS is often described as the perfect cathedral city, in that it remains a comparatively small town utterly dominated by the graceful bulk of the cathedral. It has nevertheless a distinct life of its own as a market centre. Markets are held in the picturesque square (*above*) immediately in front of the entrance to the cathedral close, which is now used as a car park. The gateway in the background is known as Penniless Porch; it is one of three main gateways linking the town, the palace and the cathedral and attributed to the middle of the fifteenth century. The Bishop's Palace, of which the embattled entrance gateway is shown (*left*) with a portion of the still well-filled moat, was the work of Bishop Jocelin, who was responsible for the major rebuilding of the cathedral in the Early English style of Gothic architecture.

74

GLASTONBURY

GLASTONBURY is a large village rather than a town and yet one of the most historic places in England. The tradition is that St. Joseph of Arimathea was responsible for the foundation of a Christian church at Glastonbury. He is said to have planted his staff in the ground; a thorn tree sprang from the staff and bloomed regularly on Christmas Day, that is, the old Christmas Day, now 6 January. Credence is given to the legend by the fact that there is at Glastonbury today a thorn tree which regularly flowers about Christmas time. Whatever the truth of the legend, there is evidence of a church on the site long before the Saxon invaders swept Christianity from the kingdom. It was St. Dunstan who founded a Benedictine abbey before the Norman occupation, though this was destroyed by a great fire in 1184. After that a new and larger abbey was constructed, of which the present fragmentary remains are a part. *Above:* Through the lofty arches of the ruined church there is seen the abbot's kitchen, an octagonal building dating from about 1440 and now used as a museum. *Below:* The beautifully moulded north door of the Norman chapel: it is surmounted by unusual moulding depicting scenes from the New Testament.

ONE OF THE MANY GEORGIAN CRESCENTS OF BATH

THE ANCIENT CITY OF BATH

BATH, today a growing residential and industrial town, has the longest continuous history as a spa of any city in England. In the later days of the Roman occupation its baths were famous. Substantial remains of this first Roman city survive. The medieval city grew up round the abbey church. In the eighteenth century the glories of the spa were revived, under the aegis of Richard (Beau) Nash, most notable of the Masters of Ceremonies, who virtually ruled the social life of Bath for several decades. In this period Bath became one of the chief fashionable centres of Britain and was largely rebuilt by the architects Woods, father and son, in a graceful but flamboyant Georgian style The pictures on this page show Pulteney Bridge (*above*) and a view of the abbey church across the Avon (*right*).

77

BRADFORD-ON-AVON

BRADFORD-ON-AVON is one of the traditional centres of Wiltshire textile manufacture. The chief factor in the historic background of Bradford was its proximity to the great wool-producing areas of the Mendips, the Cotswold and the Wiltshire Downs, together with its position on the River Avon, which linked it with Bath and Bristol. Unlike most of these ancient manufacturing centres, Bradford has preserved its tradition. A large modern mill by the riverside, shown here, provides evidence of this. Behind it rises the modern residential quarter built on terraces up the hillside.

A PICTURESQUE CORNER

BRADFORD has largely been rebuilt to keep pace with the needs of its modern industry. Graceful public buildings and well-designed blocks of shops, offices and warehouses, such as those shown here, have taken the place of the sixteenth- and seventeenth-century houses on their site, but the narrow streets of the old town remain. Only the main street has been re-designed. Bradford is also famous for the tiny Church of St. Lawrence which is of Saxon workmanship throughout, and for the medieval chapel on the bridge over the River Avon.

EXETER CATHEDRAL

EXETER is a city which possesses many links with the past, including the ruins of its medieval castle, known as Rougemont Castle, on the site of which there has been a fortress since the eleventh century, and the Guildhall, which is one of the most ancient secular buildings in Britain, dating from various periods between the fourteenth and sixteenth centuries. The city's chief pride, however, is the cathedral, which apart from the towers is almost entirely in the Decorated style of Gothic architecture. The two towers are Norman in design and largely Norman in detail and conceived with exceptional beauty. The repetition of the semi-circular arch form in the detail of the external fabric is unusually effective. The cathedral, like many other old buildings in Exeter, was damaged by aerial bombardment during the Second World War but it has few permanent scars from the ordeal.

BRISTOL—HISTORIC CENTRE

WITH a population which is now almost 450,000 and has increased within twenty years from under 400,000, Bristol is likely soon to join the select band of cities with more than half a million inhabitants. Few who pass through the busy centre of the town today would suspect its ancient history or its past glories, the accent is so entirely on the modern, the commercial and the industrial. Aerial bombardment in the Second World War razed to the ground a large part of the central area. The rebuilding of this devastated region adds still more to the air of modernity, especially the beautifully designed civic centre with its surrounding open space. Down by the harbour, too, where the docks abut on the busiest part of the city, there has been much rebuilding and many of the older houses have been

AND MODERN CITY

replaced. Yet nearly a thousand years ago Bristol was even then one of the principal towns of England. It possessed a strong castle and an abbey which flourished until the dissolution. Two Norman archways still extant formed part of the abbey gatehouse. The castle has entirely disappeared. It was the prison home of King Stephen in 1141 and was kept in repair until the great Civil War, but at the close of hostilities was "slighted" by the Parliamentarians. Thereafter its fabric was used for building houses or roads. The cathedral is the most ancient building in modern Bristol. Originally the church of the abbey, it was founded soon after the turn of the eleventh century and was largely rebuilt between 1300 and 1350. To this rebuilding most of the present choir belongs, though the Lady Chapel is older.

DORCHESTER: CAPITAL TOWN OF DORSET

OLD PORTS OF DEVONSHIRE

Both Totnes (*above*) and Teignmouth (*below*) are ancient ports, the former a river port on the River Dart, which is still navigable to this point, the latter, as its name suggests, at the mouth of the Teign. Totnes is a town whose houses are still mainly clustered within its ancient gates, of which two, the North Gate and the East Gate, are more or less intact. The fine late Gothic church is close beside the East Gate. The prominent tower of this church, in the background on the right (*above*), is a landmark which rises high above the other buildings of the town and is clearly visible five miles or more away across the rolling countryside of South Devon. Old Teignmouth lies on the river side of the long spit of land seen on the right of the photograph below. The modern town, which has a population of more than 10,000, is built up the hill behind and along the sea front of the spit. The former commercial trade of Teignmouth docks has virtually ceased, as the town's character has changed from that of a port to that of a holiday resort and residential area. In the season there are scores of pleasure boats and yachts and a few fishing boats moored there.

RIVER PORTS OF THE TAW AND TORRIDGE

BIDEFORD (*above*) and Barnstaple (*below*) are two of the most distinguished of the old river ports of North Devon. The former is on the Torridge, and the latter on the Taw. Both were flourishing and ever-increasing ports from the fourteenth century onwards, with a large export in wool. Both suffered eclipse when the railways brought alternative means of transport, and later improved roads and with them motor lorries provided further intensive competition for seaborne traffic. Until the middle of the eighteenth century at least nine-tenths of the merchandise of England's south-western counties was carried by sea, while the sea route between any two places was frequently the quickest and cheapest. Both ports, however, are exceptional in that they have retained a place as ports in the modern scheme of communications sufficient to give their watersides a busy and prosperous appearance. Finally, both towns have the distinction of a medieval many-arched bridge, built in the thirteenth century. That of Barnstaple has sixteen arches, that of Bideford twenty-four. Both have been remodelled to enable them to carry the heavy modern motor traffic but both still remain indisputably medieval in both design and construction.

BRIXHAM HARBOUR

BRIXHAM, which lies at the opposite end of Torbay to Torquay has become a modest holiday resort during the last century. As a port it no longer has commercial importance, though fishing is still carried on from it and numerous fishing boats are often at their moorings in the harbour mingled with a great number of yachts and pleasure boats. Before the decay of the coast-wise shipping traffic, however, Brixham was one of the most flourishing of the ports in South Devon and handled much of the agricultural produce of the rich area to the east of the River Dart. Brixham, too, has a special place in history as the port at which William of Orange, William III of England, landed in 1688. The statue (right) of William set up appropriately on the harbour wall, commemorates his landing on 5 November. Today Brixham has both lifeboat and coastguard stations.

PORT ON A CREEK

KINGSBRIDGE, picturesquely situated at the head of a long narrow arm of the sea, is yet another of the chain of ancient ports which flourished along the South Devon coast before the era of good roads and railway transport. Its trade was principally concerned with the agricultural products of the South Hams. *Below* is a characteristic view of the creek at high water. At low water a wide expanse of mud is revealed and there is no harbour for modern steamships. Kingsbridge, however, retains one link with its historic past, the July Fair. During the fair a stuffed glove is "hung" outside the town hall (*left*) as a token of the welcome extended to visitors. Traditionally prosecution for minor offences was suspended during the fair and the glove was "hung" as a public symbol of this special immunity.

PORCH OF THE CHURCH OF ST. MARY MAGDALENE, LAUNCESTON

PLYMOUTH'S LINKS WITH THE PAST

THE original harbour of old Plymouth is to the east of the modern town in Sutton Pool (pictured *above*) reached through the Cattewater. Here are shown the Barbican and the old Custom House. This harbour is still used by fishing boats whose catches are landed on the quayside and auctioned there. *Below* is a general view of the Hoe taken from the citadel. It was here that tradition records that Sir Francis Drake was playing bowls when news of the approach of the Spanish Armada was brought. Drake insisted on completing the game, it is said, before giving orders to man the ships, probably because he knew there was time to spare before he could take the weather station against the Spaniards. In this picture, to the right of the centre, can be seen the statue of Sir Francis Drake and beyond it, farther to the right, the Royal Naval War Memorial, similar to those at Chatham and Southsea. Another memorial, embodying part of the structure of Smeaton's original stone-built Eddystone Lighthouse, underlines Plymouth's long seafaring traditions.

PLYMOUTH, THE LIDO

ALONE among the medieval ports of South Devon, Plymouth has maintained and even added to its importance in modern times. One of the most famous of British ports in Queen Elizabeth's day, it can still so be described. Because of its magnificent natural harbours and the extensive protective works which have been carried out it is one of the chief ports of call for transatlantic shipping as well as a great naval base and commercial port. Its population, including the two old towns of Stonehouse and Devonport, is approaching a quarter of a million. During the Second World War Plymouth was the target of many enemy air raids. A great deal of both the business and residential parts of the city was razed to the ground and is now being rebuilt. Plymouth has kept pace with modern trends, as this bathing station, constructed in the shelter of the cliffs under the Hoe between the two world wars and since extended, shows. It entertains thousands of visitors during the summer months. Plymouth Sound is itself a natural harbour; the principal modern docks are in Millbay, an inlet of the Sound, while there are other extensive harbours in the Hamoaze to the west beyond Devonport (the estuary of the Tamar) which is now one of Britain's greatest naval bases, and in the Cattewater to the east, which is formed by the estuary of the Plym. Drake's Island, named after Sir Francis Drake of Spanish Armada fame, is one of the principal defence points covering the inner harbours and has been fortified for centuries.

OLD HARBOUR, LOOE

CORNWALL, like Devonshire, has a large number of old ports, a few having been in continuous use since Celtic times. Almost all have been depressed by the change from sea transport to carriage by land, but some still continue as ports in their own right. Looe (*left*) is one which has vigorously survived.

LOOE YESTERDAY AND TODAY

THE picture (*above*) shows the River Looe with the port of East Looe on the right, West Looe on the left, both having originally been independent maritime communities with a great rivalry between them. The fish market, still a vigorous part of Looe's life, is halfway along the quayside on the right. Looe now augments its revenues from the sea by catering for holidaymakers and like so many others along the Cornish coast it is thronged with visitors during the greater part of the three summer months. The picture (*right*) of a Punch and Judy performance on the sands of Looe is a speaking commentary on the change which has come over the life of this and other similar small seaports of the West Country.

ST. IVES

As Looe is to south Cornwall, so is St. Ives (*left*) to the north—a once important port which still has a small fishing fleet but owes rather more to its renown as a holiday resort than to the revenue derived from the port.

FALMOUTH ROADS

FALMOUTH'S position is rather similar to that of Padstow, though here the protection is offered by the banks of an inlet of the sea rather than by a river estuary. As a port Falmouth (*above*) only came into existence in the seventeenth century and unlike Padstow has continued to be a port in modern times, with large ship-repairing yards and other installations. Even so, it is best known as a watering place and summer holiday resort, famous for the beauty of its water front and the Fal estuary, shown here, and for its exceptional climate with very mild winters which allow some kinds of tropical plants to flourish in the open.

PENZANCE

SITUATED at the head of Mounts Bay, some eight miles to the north-east of Land's End, Penzance is the westernmost port in England. The town was re-planned late in the sixteenth century after being destroyed by Spanish raiders. It is the market centre and railhead which handles the bulk of the agricultural produce of western Cornwall and through its port come the flowers of the Scilly Isles en route to Covent Garden Market. Fishing for mackerel and pilchard once was extensive but recently there has been some decline. In the background is St. Mary's Church.

91

MAIDSTONE, AND THE RIVER MEDWAY, WITH THE BISHOP'S PALACE

South-east England

THE south and east of England have been the most densely populated areas of Britain for the greater part of recorded history. The south-east, too, is the part of the country in closest contact with Continental ideas and historically the most exposed to invasion.

Inevitably the old towns reflect both these phases of history. Those of oldest foundation were all strongly fortified while many retain parts of their medieval defences. The peaceful infiltration by Continental influence is well illustrated, for instance, by local styles of architecture such as the Dutch-style windows of early Georgian houses and by individual settlements of foreign refugees such as the weavers' homes in Canterbury.

Dover is the traditional port of entry from the Continent, a harbour which has been fortified since Roman times. It not only retains many links with the Roman fort and with the Norman and later fortifications but also preserves the tradition in its modern barracks situated on the very castle hill which has always been the centre of Dover's fortifications.

The Romans constructed the great artery of commerce which linked Dover with the Midlands and the North of England. Towns always follow trade. The large number of travellers who passed along this road, together with the need to fortify the points where the road forded the chief rivers, contributed to the growth of South-east England's other most historic towns, Canterbury, Rochester and London.

Canterbury became the religious centre of the whole realm. That was a later development which arose from the accident that it was the capital city of Ethelbert's kingdom of Kent when that enlightened sovereign was converted by the missionary, St. Augustine. Even then its strategic importance was not lost sight of. A holy city in the Middle Ages needed defences as much as any other and there are still the substantial fragments of a Norman castle, the keep of which once suffered the indignity of being used as a coal dump.

Rochester owes its existence chiefly to the fact that it lies at the point where the Medway could be forded close to its mouth. The castle and cathedral are links with its medieval importance while the town walls still standing show the hand of Roman as well as medieval builders. Rochester illustrates also another phase in the development of English towns. When the need for defence had passed and the old towns along Britain's internal trade routes were in general declining,

Rochester took on a new lease of life as the centre of a growing industrial district which includes Gillingham, Chatham and Strood, and which it is proposed to unite once more in government, as they are united in fact by economic ties, under the hybrid name of Chatchester. Its proximity to a great river gave Rochester birth; the same factor made possible this second lease of life.

London tells the same story on a far more grandiloquent scale. It, too, owed its birth to its position at the lowest point downstream at which the Thames could be forded.

London was not always the capital of England. It only attained that dignity some time after the Norman occupation. Before that Winchester was the capital, as it had been since England was united under the aegis of King Alfred.

The old towns of East Anglia tell very much the same story as those of Kent. They mostly owe their importance to their position as market centres in the Middle Ages along the main routes of communication with London and the south-east coast. The most ancient and historic of them all is Colchester, which was a tribal capital two thousand years ago and under the Romans achieved an impregnable position with special privileges as a highly Romanized centre of commerce and administration. The pagans laid waste Colchester as they did every other town of Roman Britain, but when in Norman times the town came to be rebuilt much of the building material was taken from the mouldering ruins of the Roman town.

As Colchester is to Essex, so is Norwich to Norfolk, with the additional distinction of being the religious centre of East Anglia in the Middle Ages as well as its commercial and social focus. St. Edmundsbury or, as we know it, Bury St. Edmunds, was another East Anglian city just as illustrious in the early part of the Middle Ages. It grew up round a monastery, made especially famous by the pilgrimages to the shrine of the Saxon martyr king, St. Edmund.

In an area which has such a wealth of history reflected in its towns it is difficult to select a few to typify the changing fortunes of the country through the ages. There are several old ports once of great prestige, like Rye and Winchelsea, left high and dry as the sea has receded. There are other ports like Dunwich in Suffolk which have disappeared entirely "down cliff" as the sea has advanced. There are other ports, like Blakeney in Norfolk, which are now separated from the sea by a wide belt of salt marshes.

There are the fortress towns which guard the river gaps in the South Downs country, like Lewes and Arundel, and similar fortress towns guarding gaps in the North Downs, such as Guildford and Farnham. There are cathedral cities with individual and quite different histories, such as St. Albans and Chichester. Two old towns are unique. One is Windsor, the castle home of English kings since the days of the Norman conquest. The other is Southampton.

CANTERBURY CATHEDRAL

THE great central tower of Canterbury Cathedral dominates the town, as it has done for nearly five hundred years. Now commonly known as the Bell Harry Tower, after the name of the bell hung in it, its traditional name is the Angel Steeple. It was built at the end of the fifteenth century. The first cathedral of Christchurch was founded by St. Augustine, the Roman missionary invited to the Court of the Kentish King Ethelbert in 597. A Benedictine monastery was founded at the same time and remained an important part of Canterbury's life until its dissolution in the reign of Henry VIII. As the see of the Archbishop of Canterbury, Primate of All England, the cathedral ranks first in precedence among English churches.

CANTERBURY'S GATES

THE unusual view (*above*) of the River
Stour where it flows just outside the
line of the medieval city walls to the
west of the town shows the battlemented West Gate and the Church of
Holy Cross on the right. The West
Gate is the sole surviving medieval
town gate in Canterbury. It was
rebuilt through the munificence of
Archbishop Sudbury in the last
quarter of the fourteenth century and
was the gate through which most
pilgrims to the shrine of St. Thomas
approached the city. When its useful-
ness as part of the town's defences had
ended it was used as the town gaol
and at present houses a museum.
Left is the embattled Christchurch
Gate, the main entrance to the
cathedral close, which was built as a
final enrichment of the cathedral
approaches in 1517. It suffered great
damage during riots in the Civil War.

THE DANE JOHN AND THE CITY WALL

In the foreground is one of the drum towers which are spaced at intervals along the line of the medieval city walls. Behind is the grassy mound known as the Dane John, certainly one of the most ancient sites in Canterbury, though its precise origin is still not known. Originally it was one of three similar mounds, two of them outside the city walls. These latter two were demolished when the railway station was built. The Dane John must, therefore, be regarded as a prehistoric work perhaps similar in origin and purpose to Silbury Hill which is on the Marlborough Downs.

ST. AUGUSTINE'S ABBEY GATEWAY

THE abbey of St. Augustine's was founded, like the cathedral, by St. Augustine, and became almost as powerful as the priory of Christchurch. Great rivalry existed throughout the Middle Ages between these two foundations. St. Augustine's, outside the city walls, remained throughout an independent community, its abbot owing allegiance to the Pope in Rome rather than to the Archbishop. During the last century St. Augustine's has been refounded as a training college for missionaries. The original abbey church has almost completely disappeared.

97

THE WHITE CLIFFS OF DOVER

MODERN Dover, one of South-east England's most important harbours and commercial towns, has grown up in a hollow between the downs immediately to the west of the Castle Hill, which is pictured (*above*) from the sea. Almost all that is ancient in Dover, however, is situated on Castle Hill, a position of perfect natural defence offered by the sheer chalk cliff and the steeply falling slopes of the downs. Silhouetted against the skyline in the photograph at the foot of the facing page, which was taken from the harbour, are seen from left to right, the castle with its square Norman keep, the Roman pharos or lighthouse, and the church of St. Mary in Castro. As a port Dover was first developed during the Roman occupation, though the main port of entry during those first four centuries of the Christian era was at Richborough some miles to the north-east. Dover, or as it was known, Dubris, was, however, important enough to justify the building of a road linking it with the great Roman arterial road, Watling Street, which ran from Canterbury to Rochester, London and the Midlands. On the cliff the Romans constructed the lighthouse, which was unique in Britain. Its structure has since been restored. Its purpose was probably to guide ships round the cliffs to Richborough rather than to show them the entrance to Dover harbour. In Saxon times the church of St. Mary was built adjacent to the lighthouse, its full name, St. Mary in Castro, referring to the Roman "camp" within which it was constructed. Dover came into its own in Norman times, when at the command of William of Normandy a castle with a strong square keep was built to guard the developing harbour.

HISTORIC CITY OF KENT

In its wealth of historic event the story of Rochester is second only to that of Canterbury in the county of Kent. Rochester's position at the lowest point downstream at which the Medway could be forded, assured it early importance. It was here that the Roman road Watling Street crossed the river; in the Middle Ages pilgrims from London to the shrine of St. Thomas of Canterbury normally passed through it on their way to the sacred city. A considerable Roman walled town arose in close proximity to the ford. Some fragments of the Roman walls can be traced in the later medieval ones. When the Normans came to occupy South-east England they made Rochester one of their strongholds and built the strong castle of which the square Norman keep is shown (*above, left*). This is one of the finest ruins of a Norman castle in existence and is comparable only with the castles of London (The Tower), Castle Hedingham and Norwich. The cathedral is effectively seen through one of the window openings of the castle keep (*above, right*). In spite of its mean tower and spire, Rochester cathedral is one of the most interesting of the cathedrals of the early foundation, with much solid Norman work contemporary with the castle, as well as some graceful Gothic additions. It was founded only a few years after Canterbury, when St. Augustine was organizing the whole of the south country into episcopal sees. *Below, left* is shown one of the medieval stone gateways to the cathedral close.

BUCKINGHAMSHIRE
MARKET TOWN

HIGH WYCOMBE, or as it was once known, Chipping Wycombe, is an old market town with a continuous history since Saxon days, beautifully situated in a fold of the Chiltern Hills. The furniture-making industry, once a rural craft associated with the Chiltern beech woods, is now centred in Wycombe, but it is as a market centre that this famous borough is best known. Two of its most interesting buildings recall the earlier history of its market: the Guildhall, *above*, which dates from 1757 and is on the site of an earlier guildhall, has a covered market below, while the little market house or Shambles, *right*, an eight-sided building designed by the brothers Adam, was finished in 1761.

THE PANTILES, TUNBRIDGE WELLS, KENT

OLD STREET IN HASTINGS

LIKE many other modern holiday resorts along the south and east coasts, Hastings retains the core of the ancient town. Its name proves that it was founded very early in the Anglo-Saxon period. By the time of the Norman occupation it was already a small but flourishing fishing town and seaport. The protection of its medieval castle assured its uninterrupted progress, but it was not until the nineteenth century that it began to develop as a watering place. Today the modern residential area, which includes the once separate township of St. Leonards, overshadows the "Old Town" but the latter, which stands isolated under the shadow of the cliffs, still has many of its sixteenth- and seventeenth-century buildings.

COBBLED STREETS OF RYE

THE sign of the Mermaid Inn, traditional haunt of smugglers, dominates one of the several cobbled streets in the ancient town and seaport of Rye. In the Later Middle Ages Rye was one of the most flourishing ports on the Sussex coast and an important member of the Cinque Ports Confederacy. Today it is a unique reminder of the appearance of a typical town 150 or 200 years ago, no longer commercially important, but justly proud of its ancient heritage and history.

103

ROMAN TOWN, CATHEDRAL CITY

CHICHESTER embodies the story of the typical country town from the earliest days of British history to the present and retains links with almost every period of its historic past. In turn Roman town, Saxon settlement, medieval cathedral city, Georgian market town and centre of fashion, it survives as that strange mixture of commercial activity and ecclesiastical calm which characterizes so many of England's ancient towns. It well may be that the people who founded a settlement on the present site of Chichester were emigrants from the Trundle Hill town on the downs a few miles away, of which the ramparts and ditches are still visible. Its foundation would have been a generation or two before the Roman occupation at a time when the whole accent of life in Britain was on migration from the hill towns to new valley settlements. By the time the Romans occupied southern England Chichester, or, as the Romans called it, Regnum, was a considerable tribal settlement. Roman engineers modelled its walls and drove straight roads through it at right angles to each other. These Roman roads met at the present central crossroads where the medieval market cross, in the picture opposite, was built more than a thousand years later. The cathedral, whose lofty spire and tower are shown, became the chief church in West

Sussex, a position which it has maintained from Norman times to the present day. The well-known detached bell tower also is shown on the right. The Pallant district, illustrated *left*, is the quiet area of residential streets in close proximity to the cathedral close which were rebuilt or built afresh during the quiet, decorous days of the eighteenth century. By then Chichester like many other cathedral cities of southern England had become a place in which many wealthy people retired to well-built Georgian houses, which incidentally are still occupied without any major alterations having been made to their fabric. The handsome, typically Georgian houses in the photograph on the left are on the south side of the East Pallant. Others still intact include at least one attributed to Sir Christopher Wren and several which were designed by architects inspired by the Wren tradition. The Pallant, consisting of four narrow streets meeting in the middle, is in the south-east of Chichester. In early documents the name is Palenta, signifying "within the pale of the Archbishop," the district being owned exclusively by the Archbishops of Canterbury.

LEWES, SUSSEX

LEWES owes its existence to its position at the point where the River Ouse breaks through the bulwark of the South Downs, a place on that account of special strategic importance, like Arundel (page 4). The town is centred on its castle which overlooks the modern business quarter below and commands the river gap. The first castle on the site was the work of the Earl of Surrey, a lieutenant of William of Normandy. It was rebuilt in the twelfth century, to which period the present ruins belong. After the great Civil War, like almost every other castle in the south country, it was slighted (i.e. dismantled) by order of Oliver Cromwell. There are in Lewes today also a number of quaint thoroughfares like that shown (left) with houses distinguished by the traditional Sussex hanging tiles, the equivalent of weather-boarding in East Anglia.

CHRISTCHURCH, HAMPSHIRE

THE religious and the military join forces in the early story of Christchurch, one of the oldest towns in Hampshire, lying a few miles to the east of Bournemouth. The photograph (*below*) shows the priory church, a handsome church with many Norman pillars and arches dating from the middle of the twelfth century, when it was founded along with many other Norman priories and abbeys in the south country. After the dissolution of the monasteries it became, as it is today, the parish church. Fragments of the medieval castle are scanty but on the right of the picture below are the ruins of the constable's house, which is sometimes called the Norman house (notice the round-headed window openings). On the right is part of the handsome Gothic cloister of the priory. In the Middle Ages Christchurch had trade by sea but the harbour silted up.

THE CATHEDRAL AND TOWN OF WINCHESTER

WINCHESTER lies in a hollow of the Hampshire downs where the River Itchen has cut a steep-sided valley through the chalk. In ancient times it was the first city of England, the capital of King Alfred's kingdom of Wessex, and shared with London the capital's privileges until well after the Norman occupation. The cathedral, which is here seen from west to east, is one of the longest medieval churches in Christendom, well over five hundred feet from the east end of the choir to the west end of the nave. It was one of the early Norman foundations following King Alfred's Saxon church and the monastery which he founded. Much Norman work remains in the fabric which, however, has been enlarged and rebuilt several times and now shows fine examples of every medieval style of building. Apart from Alfred the Great the most illustrious name connected with the town is that of William of Wykeham, the famous fourteenth-century scholar and divine who was bishop from 1367 until his death in 1404 and was responsible for the last and most magnificent rebuilding of the cathedral and for the foundation of Winchester College. Today Winchester, though fallen from its metropolitan importance, remains the county town of Hampshire, an assize town and a market centre for a vast area of thinly peopled Hampshire down country. Its castle, close by the West Gate, was the birthplace of Henry III. It has been dismantled.

↑ The Eclipse, not God Begot House
Hotel's the other side of the High St.

SCENES FROM OLD WINCHESTER

THE statue of King Alfred (*above, right*) is at the lower end of the High Street. It was erected to the design of H. Thornycroft in 1901 to mark the millennium of the traditional date of King Alfred's death. The God Begot House (*above, left*) is one of the oldest of Winchester's ancient houses, now licensed as an inn and carefully preserved in its entirety. Many of the timber beams and part of the doorway shown here are original. The City Cross (*right*) designed in the style of the Eleanor Crosses, is in an alcove halfway up the High Street and is flanked by a piazza or colonnade in which the upper storeys of the houses are supported by pillars, giving a covered walk along what is now a row of shops.

109

MARLBOROUGH HIGH STREET

THE unusually broad High Street of Marlborough (*below*) forms part of the main highway from London to Bath and is a popular "port of call" for travellers between the east and the west country. So broad is the High Street that Marlborough's market is held in its centre, as shown (*left*). Marlborough's greatest interest is that it is one of the few English towns built in a homogeneous style of architecture. Many of the houses and other buildings which flank the main street were built within fifty years of the disastrous fire of 1635, which ranks among the most damaging holocausts that any English town has suffered. Several of the present hotels show indisputable signs of having been coaching inns, but the most famous of them all, the Castle Inn, has become a public school.

SOUTHAMPTON, THE HIGH STREET AND BARGATE

THERE are three distinct phases in Southampton's history. The first is as a medieval walled town, the second as a prosperous commercial and trading centre of the seventeenth and eighteenth centuries, the most recent as one of Britain's largest and most flourishing ports, with great importance as the terminus for many of the great transatlantic liners. Southampton, too, has suffered one great catastrophe, the intensive bombing by enemy aircraft during the Second World War, when great damage was done to the port and a large part of the main shopping thoroughfare and the most ancient and historic part of the town was blasted or destroyed by subsequent fires. Repairs to the docks were quickly completed and a fine start has been made on rebuilding the town, but the completion of this work will occupy many years to come. The photograph (*above*) is looking up the comparatively undamaged part of the High Street to the Bargate, the surviving town gate. A part of the medieval town walls are also extant and have further been revealed by demolition consequent on the bombing. Modern Southampton dates from the foundation of the docks in 1838. The docks passed into the control of the railways fifty years later and were continuously developed up to the period immediately preceding the Second World War. The famous King George V Dock, which is described as the largest dry dock in the world, was opened only in 1935. Despite the tricky tides and currents of the Solent the sheltered natural harbour of the town was much in demand even in the Middle Ages.

SALISBURY TODAY

In the thirteenth century the monks of the abbey at Old Sarum decided that its site on the Wiltshire Downs was unduly exposed and impracticable of further development. So they migrated *en masse* to the valley, where within fifty years they had completed the construction of the only ancient cathedral in England which is predominantly of one style of architecture, the delicately graceful style of Gothic known as Early English. Around the abbey, as so often happened, there grew up a market town, and on the page *opposite* is shown the market cross still serving, as it has done for many centuries, to give shelter to the stall keepers and housewives of Salisbury and the surrounding district. The view of the cathedral shown (*above*) is the famous one from Constable's "Rainbow Bridge".

GUILDFORD, COUNTY TOWN OF SURREY

THE cobbled high street, flanked by the Guildhall and many old houses and inns, slopes down
to the valley of the Wey; the green hills seen beyond are those of the North Downs.

TWO CASTLES OF SURREY

THE photograph (*below*) shows Farnham's Castle Street leading to the reconstructed castle. On the right is the medieval keep of the castle of Guildford built in Norman times to protect the valley of the Wey. This castle had an uneventful history and at the end of the great Civil War was left to moulder in ruins. The castle of Farnham, by contrast, has a continuous history as a residence—part castle, part palace. As ancient as that of Guildford (its keep was built in the twelfth century), it was entirely reconstructed in the seventeenth century and until 1926 was one of the palaces of the Bishops of Winchester, after which date when the diocese of Guildford was formed it passed into the usage of the Bishops of Guildford. Both of these country towns with their many survivals from the Middle Ages are to some extent protected from rapid change by the by-pass roads which leave their narrow High Streets for the use of townspeople.

ROYAL WINDSOR

WINDSOR is a town whose story has always been subordinate to that of its castle, which still dominates its streets and its riverside, as it has done for more than a thousand years. The three views on these pages show different phases in the castle's history. The photograph *above* shows the well-loved view from the River Thames, with the Round Tower prominent in the main mass of the castle buildings. *Opposite, below,* is the "Norman" gateway leading from the central ward to the lower ward and (*above*) the graceful perpendicular Gothic lines of St. George's Chapel, better known, perhaps, as the chapel of the Order of the Garter. There was a castle at Windsor before the Conquest, but it was William of Normandy who founded what was to become the principal residence of the kings of England, combining the functions of a royal palace with those of a castle to defend the important waterway of the Thames. The Thames, too, served as a moat on two sides of the castle bluff, which was itself well suited for defence. Its proximity to London also enhanced the royal value of Windsor Castle. So it is not surprising that it quickly became the acknowledged headquarters of the sovereign and has sheltered practically every king and queen since Norman times. Little of the original Norman building survives except the lower storeys of the Round Tower, which was elevated incongruously by the architect Wyatville in the early part of the last century. The greater part of the present state apartments in the upper ward date from Restoration times, though much of the exterior of these too was remodelled by Wyatville. St. George's Chapel, however, owes nothing to modern restoration. It was built mainly in the quarter-century between 1475 and 1500.

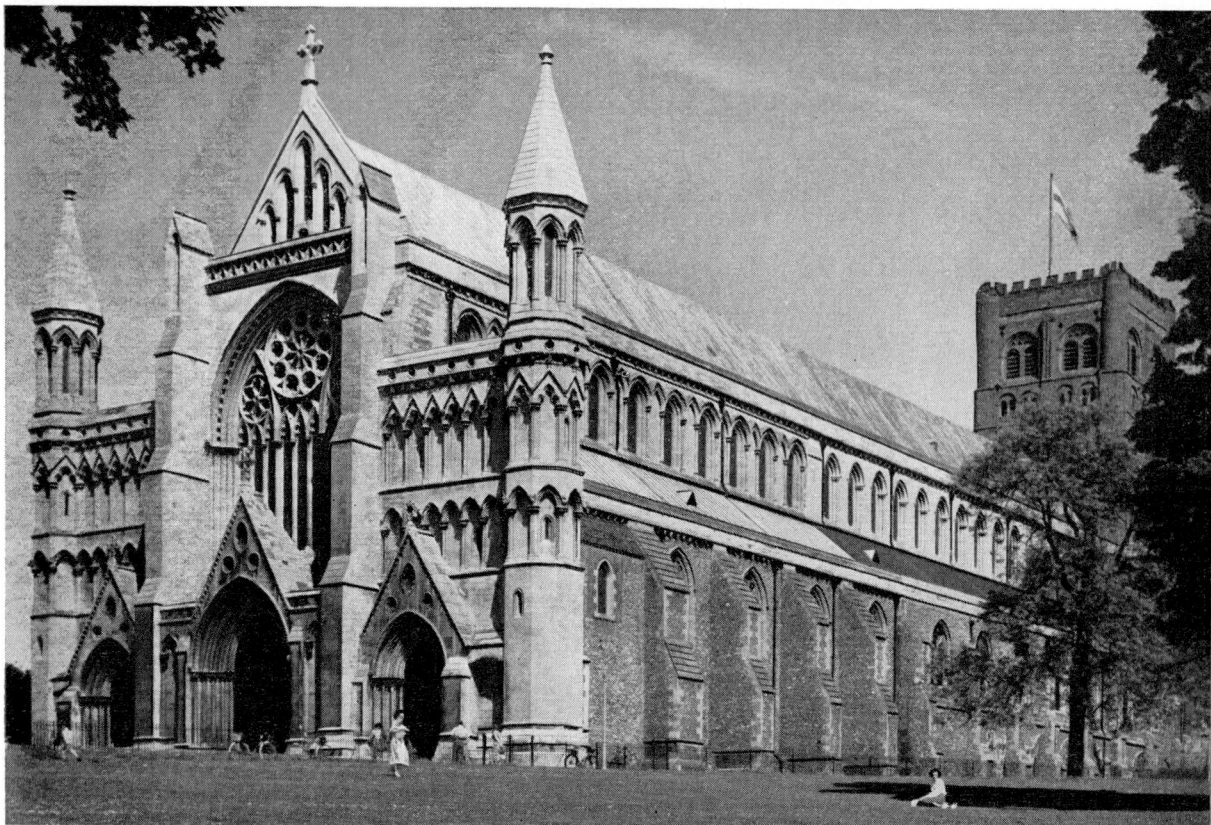

THE CITY OF ST. ALBANS

THE abbey of St. Albans was founded on the site on which the first English martyr, Albanus, was crucified for his adherence to the faith, when the Roman town of Verulamium, situated on the lower ground to the south, was nearing the end of its four centuries of prosperity under Roman rule. The abbey in turn became unusually prosperous and the town of St. Albans grew up round it, a trading and market centre dependent on the abbot for its very existence. After the dissolution in the reign of King Henry VIII the town continued to grow (its narrow streets retain many seventeenth-century houses, *left*). Today it combines the dignity of a cathedral city (the abbey church has become the cathedral) with the bustle and commotion of a busy market centre.

118

TWO TOWNS OF HERTFORDSHIRE

BISHOP'S STORTFORD and Hertford (*below*) are representative of the many quiet country towns to the north and north-east of the metropolis. Both are ancient towns situated at a ford, each with a castle guarding that ford, in the case of Bishop's Stortford the ford over the River Stort, in the case of Hertford over the River Lea. Both have fine churches rebuilt during the century before the Reformation. Both towns have a number of houses dating from the sixteenth and seventeenth centuries and a few of Jacobean craftsmanship.

THE CASTLE AND DOCKS OF COLCHESTER

COLCHESTER, set on a hill above the River Colne, from which it takes its name, is the most historic town of eastern Essex. It was a Roman walled town; it was an important Saxon settlement; and then one of the largest of the Norman towns in the east. The massive castle (*above*), now used as a museum, was built in Norman times though its fabric is largely composed of the thin red Roman bricks which were taken by its builders from the ruins of the Roman town. From the twelfth century until about two hundred years ago Colchester flourished as a market centre and as a port, the Colne being navigable by sailing vessels to this point. Today it remains a large and still-growing market centre and unlike so many of Britain's river ports still has a sizable trade passing through its docks (*left*) which are used by the sailing barges which continue to ply up the Thames and along the east coast of England.

120

BURY ST. EDMUNDS TODAY AND YESTERDAY

THE two pictures show St. Edmundsbury, the cathedral city of Suffolk as it is today (*below*) and as it was in 1898. The two pictures show the same view with the abbey gateway in the left foreground and the church of St. James (the cathedral of the present diocese of St. Edmundsbury and Ipswich) in the background. The picture above gives some idea of the immense wealth of the Benedictine Abbey of Bury in the Middle Ages and of the vast extent of its buildings and its adjacent churches (even the cathedral, which only dates from the fifteenth century, was built from the abbot's funds). The secret of this great foundation's wealth was that until the dissolution the abbots of Bury were the lords of the manor and the sole landlords of the thriving town with its immense trade in wool, as they were also the sole licensees of the town's markets and fairs. So great was popular feeling against the extortions of the abbot that during the Peasants' Revolt the rebels destroyed part of the abbey buildings by fire and murdered the abbot and many of his chief officers. St. Edmundsbury takes its name from Edmund, martyr king of East Anglia, who was slain by Viking warriors in the ninth century and whose body was buried in Bury's monastery. Therein lay another source of wealth for the monks derived from the many thousands of pilgrims who throughout the Middle Ages came each year to worship at the shrine of St. Edmund.

A TOWN OF NORTHERN ESSEX

SAFFRON WALDEN has many claims to be considered among the most interesting towns in Essex. It has largely preserved its former quietness, since it lies well away from the present line of the main road linking London and East Anglia. It has changed little, too, within living memory because no great development followed the Industrial Revolution and though served by a branch railway line it was not well placed either with regard to transport or raw materials. It has remained, therefore, primarily a market town frequented by the country folk of northern Essex and by the people living in a wider area between Cambridge and Bishop's Stortford. Its pride is its magnificent fifteenth-century church, a landmark for miles around. This is one of the wool churches comparable in Essex only with that of Thaxted, lofty in the true Perpendicular style of Gothic, presenting a finely moulded, beautifully proportioned exterior but relatively poor and without decoration inside. Saffron Walden lies on a spur of the chalk hills known as the East Anglian Heights, a specially favoured region for sheep pasture in the later Middle Ages. Consequently Saffron Walden itself was a great centre of weaving and an important wool market. The projecting upper storeys of some sixteenth- and seventeenth-century houses can be seen towards the lower end of the street shown here. Even earlier than that Saffron Walden, which derives its name from the saffron flower which for long has been extensively cultivated in the district, was a place of notable importance, to which fact the ivy-covered remains of the now ruined castle, which the Normans built to dominate the town, bear witness.

IN OLD KING'S LYNN

THIS is yet another of Britain's ancient seaports whose commerce diminished when steam took the place of sail and railways and road robbed shipping of much of its traditional carrying trade. Yet even now it is one of the largest and most prosperous of Norfolk's many towns, its historic heritage unusually obvious in its wealth of old buildings, its modern prosperity typified by the fine shopping thoroughfare and, above all, by the markets which are the hub of King's Lynn's life today, as they have been for five hundred years. From time immemorial Lynn has been licensed to hold two markets, one on Saturday and one on Tuesday, each in its own market place. *Below* is shown the Tuesday market in full swing. South Gate (*right*) is the only surviving part of the medieval mural defences.

GREAT YARMOUTH

LIKE Teignmouth (page 83) Great Yarmouth faces two ways, eastward towards the sea and westward towards the River Yare, the town itself being built on a long narrow spit of land separating the two. There is nothing in common between these two faces of one of the oldest towns and one of the largest in East Anglia. To the east it presents the aspect of a typical holiday resort. On the riverside it is a port and an important one at that, at its busiest in the herring fishing season. At the south end of its long spit of land lies the area known as the South Denes, with the fish wharves adjoining. The photograph (*below*) shows the fisher girls (many of whom come south each year from Scotland) packing barrels with fish for consignment to all parts of the continent. Of the medieval town walls several parts remain intact, including three of the original drum towers, of which one is shown in the photograph on the left.

FORGOTTEN TOWNS OF EAST ANGLIA

THE towns pictured on this page are Maldon (*above*) and Fakenham (*below*). Maldon and Fakenham, though they stand at opposite ends of the ancient province of East Anglia, Maldon on one of the eastern estuaries of Essex, Fakenham in the north-west corner of Norfolk, have one thing in common, that their historic fame has not been matched by their growth in the nineteenth and twentieth centuries. Yet both are still flourishing. Maldon was once a port which was at the height of its importance from the fourteenth cen-

tury to the seventeenth century. When most goods were transported by water, Maldon's position on the Blackwater estuary made it a perfect haven for the sailing ships and sailing barges which plied round the coast of Britain and across the seas to the Low Countries and France. Like the coast-wise ports of Devon and Cornwall, it decayed only when railway and road competed seriously with transport by sea. Fakenham, by contrast, has always been a market town first and foremost. Unlike Maldon, it derived its importance from its position at the natural meeting-place of the old roads which cross north Norfolk and it remains an important market and shopping centre.

125

THE CAPITAL OF EAST ANGLIA

NORWICH has been the true capital of East Anglia since the Norman conquest and is still the largest and most flourishing town in the region. The cathedral was begun in the eleventh century, the greater part of it being completed before the middle of the twelfth century. Many visitors regard the view of the cathedral from Mousehold Heath (*opposite, top*) as the most beautiful distant view of any English cathedral. The market of Norwich (*below*) typifies the importance of Norwich as the centre of one of Britain's richest agricultural countrysides. It is a market, too, in fact as well as in name, though the cattle market, which is one of the largest of its kind in the kingdom, has been moved to a different site. Among the buildings seen in this picture are the old Guildhall, right, a building dating from Tudor England, and the glaringly modern, but not unsuccessful, classical architecture of the new City Hall, left, with its conspicuous clock tower. In spite of some damage from bombs during the Second World War, many of Norwich's old streets remain more or less intact; among them are Bridewell Lane and Swan Lane (*opposite, below*).

INDEX

(Figures in italics signify pictures)

Abingdon, *42*
Alnwick, *17*
Arundel, *4, 94*

Bamburgh, *17*
Banbury, *37*
Barnstaple, 71, 72, *84*
Bath, *2,* 72, *76, 77*
Berwick-on-Tweed, 14, *19*
Bideford, 71, *84*
Birmingham, 32
Bishop's Stortford, *119*
Blackburn, 14
Bradford-on-Avon, *78*
Bristol, *80, 81*
Brixham, *85*
Burford, *43*
Burnley, 14
Bury St. Edmunds, 94, *121*

Cambridge, 32, *50, 51*
Canterbury, 93, *85, 96, 97*
Carlisle, 14, *18*
Chatham, 94
Cheltenham, *63*
Chepstow, *67*
Chester, 14, *24, 25*
Chichester, 94, *104, 105*
Chipping Campden, 54, *55*
Christchurch, *107*
Cirencester, 54, *56*
Colchester, 94, *120*
Coventry, *36*

Derby, 13, *48, 49*
Dorchester, *82*
Dover, 93, *98, 99*
Dunwich, 94
Durham, 14, *15*

Ely, *7,* 31
Evesham, 54, *59*
Exeter, 71, *79*

Fakenham, *125*
Falmouth, *91*
Farnham, 94, *115*

Gillingham, 94
Glastonbury, 72, *75*
Gloucester, 53, 54, *62*
Great Yarmouth, *124*
Grimsby, 27
Guildford, 94, *114, 115*

Hastings, *103*
Hereford, 53, *61*
Hertford, *119*
High Wycombe, *101*
Huntingdon, *46*

Kendal, 14
Kingsbridge, 71, *86*
King's Lynn, *123*

Lancaster, 14, *26*
Launceston, 71, *87*
Ledbury, *52*
Leicester, 13, 31, *44*
Lewes, 94, *106*
Lichfield, *30,* 32
Lincoln, 13, *28, 29*
Looe, 71, *90*
Ludlow, *68*

Maidstone, *92*
Maldon, *125*
Manchester, 14
Market Harborough, 32
Marlborough, *110*
Monmouth, 53, 54, *69*
Moreton-in-the-Marsh, *58*

Newark-upon-Trent, *47*
Newcastle-upon-Tyne, 14, *16*
Newport, 54
Norwich, 94, *126, 127*
Nottingham, *9,* 13, 31

Oakham, 31, *45*
Oldham, 14
Oxford, 32, *39, 40, 41*

Padstow, 71
Penzance, 72, *91*
Pershore, 54
Peterborough, *49*
Plymouth, 72, *88, 89*

Richmond, 14, *23*
Ripon, 14, *22*
Rochester, 93, 94, *100*
Rye, 94, *103*

Saffron Walden, *122*
St. Albans, 94, *118*
St. Ives (Cornwall), 71, *90*
St. Ives (Hunts), 31, *46*
Salisbury, *112, 113*
Shrewsbury, 53, 54, *60*
Southampton, 94, *111*
Stamford, 13, *33*
Stow-on-the-Wold, *57*
Stratford-upon-Avon, 32
Strood, 94

Teignmouth, *83*
Tewkesbury, *66*
Totnes, *83*
Truro, *70*
Tunbridge Wells, *102*

Uppingham, 32

Warwick, 32, *34, 35*
Wells, *73, 74*
Whitby, 13
Winchelsea, 94
Winchester, *108, 109*
Windsor, 94, *116, 117*
Worcester, 54, *64-5*

York, 13, 14, *20, 21*

First published 1957
Made and printed in Great Britain by Odhams (Watford) Ltd., Watford
Copyright T.357.Q.

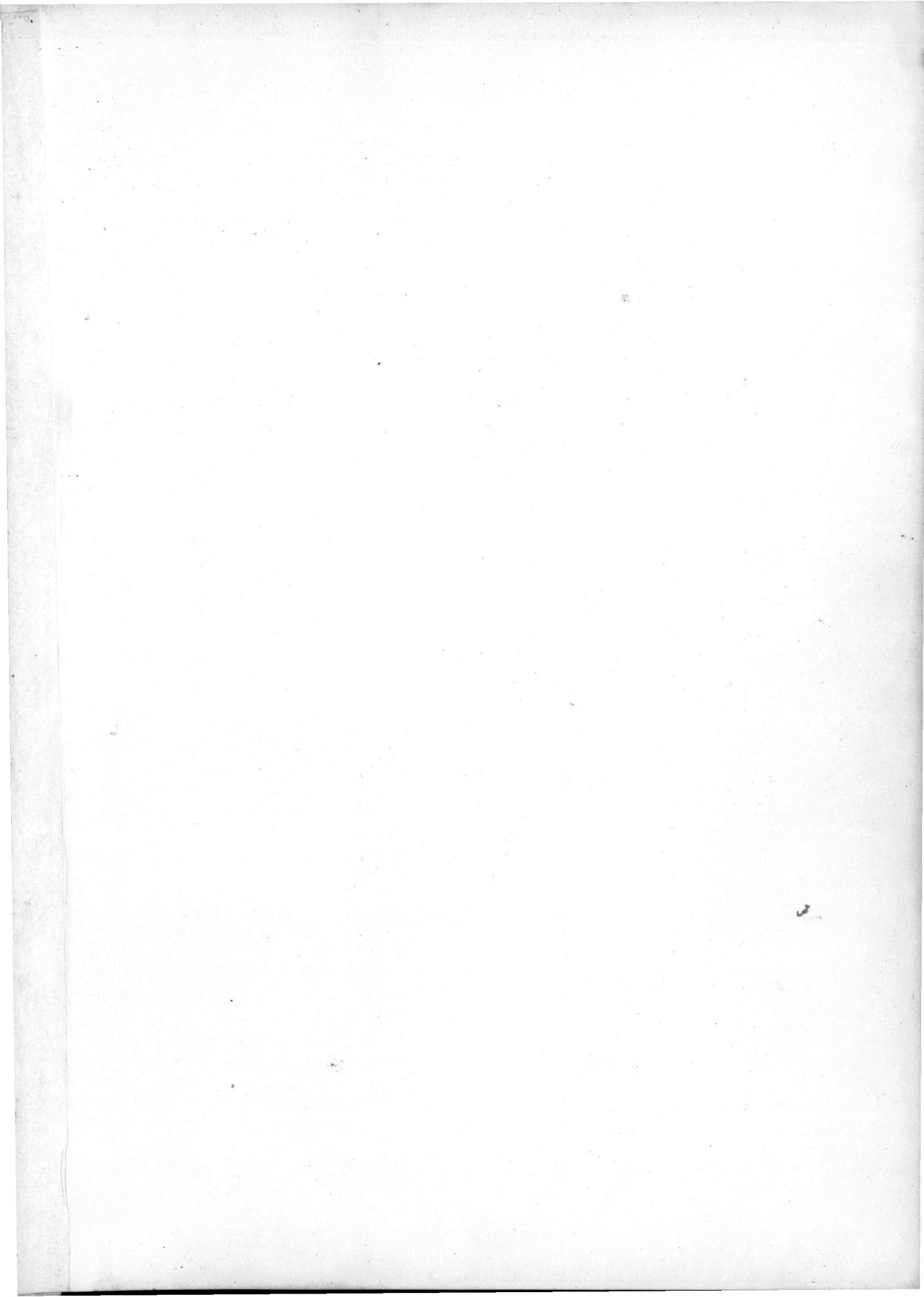